from
DOG BRIDEGROOM
to WOLF GIRL

SERIES IN FAIRY-TALE STUDIES

GENERAL EDITOR
Donald Haase, Wayne State University

ADVISORY EDITORS

A complete listing of the books in this series can be found online at wsupress.wayne.edu

from
DOG BRIDEGROOM
to WOLF GIRL

Contemporary

Japanese Fairy-Tale

Adaptations

in Conversation

with the West

MAYAKO MURAI

WAYNE STATE UNIVERSITY PRESS | DETROIT

19 18 17 16 15   5 4 3 2 1

ISBN 978-0-8143-3949-7 (paperback)
ISBN 978-0-8143-3950-3 (ebook)

Library of Congress Control Number: 2015945037

Published with the assistance of a fund established by Thelma Gray James
of Wayne State University for the publication of folklore and English studies.

Designed and typeset by Bryce Schimanski
Composed in Adobe Caslon Pro

CONTENTS

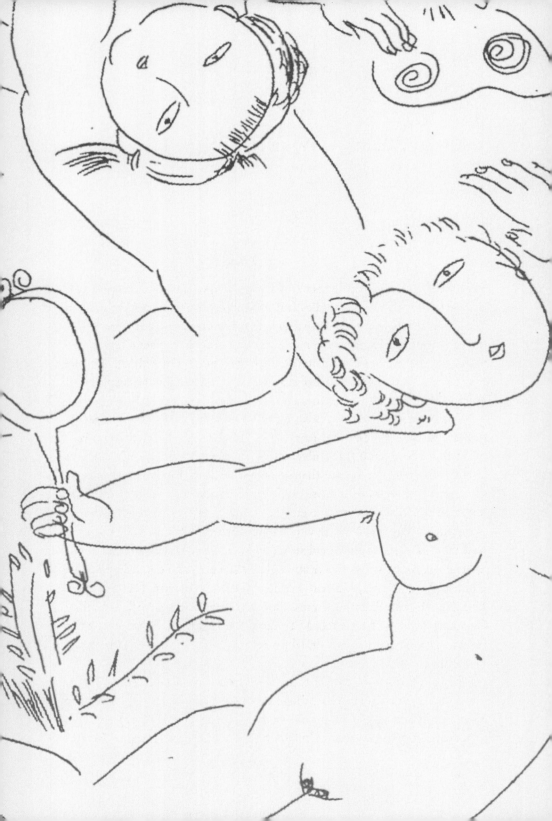

ACKNOWLEDGMENTS

My deepest gratitude first goes to my mentor Sugiyama Yōko for introducing me both to fairy-tale studies and to feminist literary criticism back in 1991, when I was in my third year at university. Reading Jack Zipes's *Victorian Fairy Tales: The Revolt of the Fairies and Elves* in her seminar opened up for me the whole field of intellectual engagement with this simple narrative form. I am, therefore, also grateful to Jack Zipes for the inspirations provided by his many works in the field.

The basic idea for this book was first formed after I gave a presentation at the conference "The Fairy Tale After Angela Carter" organized by Stephen Benson at the University of East Anglia in 2009. It came as a wonderful surprise to me that several participants expressed enthusiasm for my analysis of the uses of Western fairy tales in contemporary Japanese art. Since then, conversations with scholars, writers, and artists from various parts of the world have deepened my understanding of how fairy tales travel across cultures and have helped me shape this book. Special mention is due to Cristina Bacchilega, Luciana Cardi, Jazmina Cininas, Lucy Fraser, Donald Haase, Martine Hennard Dutheil de la Rochère, Higami Kumiko, Vanessa Joosen, Anna Kérchy, Gillian Lathey, Catriona McAra, Margaret Mitsutani, John Patrick Pazdziora, Stijn Praet, Michelle Ryan-Sautour, Marc Sebastian-Jones, and Francisco Vaz da Silva.

Many thanks also to the three anonymous readers of this book in manuscript, who gave me invaluable advice (the word *conversation* in the subtitle was suggested by one of these readers), and to the remarkable team at Wayne State University Press, especially Annie Martin for her generous support and attentive overseeing of the publication process, Kristina E. Stonehill for her help with the rights, and Robin DuBlanc for her thorough editing of the manuscript. Working with them was a rewarding, enlightening, and pleasurable experience for me.

The chapter on Kōnoike Tomoko is especially important to me because, in the process of writing this book, the artist and I began to collaborate on a new project combining art and fairy-tale research. I am grateful to her for sharing her intense curiosity about fairy tales with me.

Some of the ideas in this book have been explored in my earlier publications; I would like to thank the editors of the following journals and edited books in which my work appeared: "Guro-Kawaii Re-envisionings of Fairy Tales in Contemporary Japanese Art," in *Postmodern Reinterpretations of Fairy Tales: How Applying New Methods Generates New Meanings*, ed. Anna Kérchy (New York: Edwin Mellen, 2011), 145–62; "In the Realm of the Senses: Tomoko Konoike's Visual Recasting of 'Little Red Riding Hood,'" in *Anti-tales: The Uses of Disenchantment*. ed. Catriona Fay McAra and David Calvin (Newcastle: Cambridge Scholars, 2011), 152–62; "In the Midst of Metamorphosis: Yōko Tawada's 'The Bridegroom Was a Dog,'" in *New Fairy Tales: Essays and Stories*, ed. John Patrick Pazdziora and Defne Çizakça (Oklahoma City: Unlocking, 2013), 281–97; "The Princess, the Witch, and the Fireside: Yanagi Miwa's Uncanny Restaging of Fairy Tales," *Marvels & Tales: Journal of Fairy-Tale Studies* 27.2 (2013): 234–53; and "Before and After the 'Grimm Boom': Re-interpretations of Grimm's Tales in Contemporary Japan," in *Grimms' Tales around the Globe: The Dynamics of Their International Reception*, ed. Vanessa Joosen and Gillian Lathey (Detroit: Wayne State UP, 2014), 153–76.

Last but not least, I would like to thank my partner, Paul Rossiter, my parents, and all the cats who have shared their lives with me for their boundless support and inspiration. Paul not only patiently read the manuscript at different stages with his poet's sensibility and editor's acumen but also has always managed to make me laugh even at my lowest ebb. I dedicate this book to him.

from
DOG BRIDEGROOM
to WOLF GIRL

INTRODUCTION

During the past three decades, the fairy tale has become an increasingly powerful inspiration for many cultural products for both adults and children in fields as diverse as literature, visual art, film, theater, dance, music, fashion, television, computer games, and architecture. This recent fairy-tale renaissance in the West is characterized by the dynamic interaction between creative adaptations and critical discourses, especially those informed by feminism: the two have been complicating, challenging, and enhancing each other. This coevolution of fairy-tale rewriting and research has been widely acknowledged. In his introduction to *Contemporary Fiction and the Fairy Tale* (2008), Stephen Benson notes "the extraordinary synchronicity, in the final decades of the twentieth century, of fiction and fairy-tale scholarship" that followed the publications in 1979 of both Angela Carter's *The Bloody Chamber and Other Stories* and Jack Zipes's *Breaking the Magic Spell: Radical Theories of Folk and Fairy Tales* (5). In *Relentless Progress: The Reconfiguration of Children's Literature, Fairy Tales, and Storytelling* (2009), Zipes observes that "[e]ver since 1980 there has been an inextricable, dialectical development of mutual influence among *all* writers of fairy tales and fairy-tale criticism that has led to innovative fairy-tale experiments in all cultural fields" (121–22). Vanessa Joosen's *Critical and Creative Perspectives on Fairy Tales: An Intertextual Dialogue between Fairy-Tale Scholarship and Postmodern Retellings* (2011) persuasively demonstrates how the dialogic interaction between literary theory and fairy-tale retellings has given an impetus to the development of the fairy-tale genre in the West.

In Japan, too, characters, motifs, and patterns derived from traditional fairy tales, many of which belong to the Western canon, have increasingly pervaded various areas of culture, especially since the 1990s.[1] As in the West, fairy-tale adaptations in contemporary Japan tend to feature female characters with a more independent spirit and display a more female-oriented perspective than traditional tales. Studio Ghibli's animation films based on Western and Japanese fairy tales, such as *Gake no ue no Ponyo* (dir. Miyazaki Hayao,[2] 2008; Ponyo on the Cliff by the Sea), an adaptation of Hans Christian Andersen's "The Little Mermaid," and *Kaguya-hime no monogatari* (dir. Takahata Isao, 2013; The Tale of the Princess Kaguya), based on the tenth-century literary fairy tale in Japan, may first come to mind. Both films revise the stereotype of passive heroines in fairy tales and depict the adventures of strong-minded, intelligent, and imaginative women. Sandra L. Beckett's study *Red Riding Hood for All Ages: A Fairy-Tale Icon in Cross-Cultural Contexts* (2008) discusses contemporary Japanese fairy-tale adaptations in media including manga, anime, a musical, a *kyōgen* (traditional Japanese comic theater) performance, and an origami (paper-folding) art book, showing the tale's versatile appeal to both children and adults in Japan. Kate Bernheimer's collection of contemporary fairy-tale retellings, *My Mother She Killed Me, My Father He Ate Me: Forty New Fairy Tales* (2010), includes two short stories by Japanese women, Awa Naoko's "First Day of Snow" and Itō Hiromi's "I Am Anjuhimeko," which offer examples of creative literary— and, in Itō's case, feminist—retellings of traditional Japanese tales.

In spite of a plethora of fairy-tale adaptations in many areas of contemporary Japanese culture, however, there has not yet appeared a substantial body of criticism dealing with the innovative ways in which each work revives and transforms elements from traditional fairy tales. It was this disparity between the prevalence of fairy-tale adaptations and the lack of critical, especially feminist, scrutiny of how fairy tales are received and transformed in contemporary Japan that motivated me to try to fill the gap by critically responding to the vigor, diversity, and complexity of fairy-tale re-creations by contemporary Japanese writers and artists. The two main questions that I will be addressing throughout this book are: What kind of criticism would be needed to analyze fairy-tale adaptations produced in a non-Western culture? What insights would such an analysis in turn bring to current fairy-tale re-creations and research in the West?

To answer these questions, this book closely examines the uses of fairy tales in the works of four contemporary Japanese women writers and artists in light of recent developments in Euro-American feminist fairy-tale scholarship. It aims to illustrate how the fairy-tale intertexts in their works, which have not yet attracted much critical attention either within or outside Japan, can inform as well as be informed by current feminist fairy-tale criticism in the West. A work may take on a new resonance when put under the scrutiny of a critical tradition different from that of its originating culture, acquiring another layer of meaning while at the same time expanding the scope of that critical tradition. This book is an attempt to perform a cross-cultural analysis that will recontextualize both cultures in a mutually illuminating way.

This project, therefore, can also be placed within a broader context of world literature studies. In his keynote lecture delivered at a conference on world literature held in Tokyo, David Damrosch observed that the exploration of what he calls the "incommensurability" of different cultural traditions plays a newly vital role in today's global literary cultures ("Comparing the Incomparable" 133). I would argue that a cross-cultural study of the fairy tale serves as a useful paradigm of a comparative method for connecting works from different traditions—from ancient and modern times and from the East and the West—through common motifs and patterns without effacing cultural incommensurability. In order to avoid falling into the essentialist trap of either universalizing fairy-tale archetypes by erasing differences or reducing differences into cultural stereotypes, I will ground my argument on a close textual analysis of the works of four women writers and artists as representing the innovative approaches to the fairy tale emerging from a non-Western culture and participating in the global circulation of cultures today.

In *Fairy Tales Transformed? Twenty-first-Century Adaptations and the Politics of Wonder* (2013), Cristina Bacchilega addresses this issue at the very end of her book, in the final note to her epilogue:

> Astutely, one of the confidential readers of this manuscript suggested I address the "'impossibility' of comparative fairy-tale studies on a global scale." This scholar asked, "How do we train the next generation of scholars?" and "Do we still need specialists in national languages and literatures, or will they be displaced by a new generation of scholars who think globally, even when it means sacrificing precision and depth?" These

questions bring home the importance of language skills and cultural knowledge in our scholarship. I hope to have championed their importance and to have been mindful of my limitations. Meeting the challenge of truly comparative fairy-tale studies may never be a reality, and my point is not to think of a worldwide fairy-tale web, but a worldly one. The process of writing this book has only intensified my conviction that collaboration across national and disciplinary boundaries is key to the future of our inquiry and conversations. (243)

My aim is precisely to meet "the challenge of truly comparative fairy-tale studies" and to emphasize the gain, rather than the loss, in adopting a cross-cultural approach. This book hopes to join in such collaborative inquiries and conversations on the interpretation of fairy tales across cultural boundaries.

The aim of this book is twofold. On the one hand, feminist fairy-tale criticism will provide an effective way of understanding contemporary Japanese literature and art, especially in terms of expressions of women's desires and experiences, which have so far been underrepresented. As I will argue in chapter 1, fairy-tale scholarship in Japan has largely failed to incorporate important insights afforded by Euro-American feminist fairy-tale criticism, a serious oversight on the part of critics working in the fields of folklore, literature, and art in Japan. On the other hand, my cross-cultural analysis will test the validity of the critical approaches to fairy-tale scholarship in the West by applying them to the examination of non-Western material and will try to identify both the limitations and the advantages of such methodologies. Such an attempt will help fairy-tale scholarship to move beyond its still mainly Western-oriented vision and, to use Bacchilega's term, to "remap" the fairy-tale genre.

Fairy Tales and Feminism: New Approaches (2004), edited by Donald Haase, has been seminal in the development of cross-cultural feminist analysis of fairy-tale rewriting that goes beyond a European and North American focus. Sandra L. Beckett's aforementioned *Red Riding Hood for All Ages* and her anthology *Revisioning Red Riding Hood around the World: An Anthology of International Retellings* (2013) include the retellings of this ever-popular tale produced in Africa, Asia, Australia, and South America. Bacchilega's *Fairy Tales Transformed?* has further expanded the cross-cultural perspective in order to "'provincialize' the Euro-American literary fairy tale" (ix). In 2013, *Marvels & Tales: Journal of Fairy-Tale Studies* published a special issue on the fairy tale in contemporary Japan, edited by Marc Sebastian-Jones under Haase's general editorship, which includes criticism and translation of some of the works by Japanese writers and artists discussed in this book. My analysis of Japanese fairy-tale adaptations owes much to these examples of cross-cultural research and aims to respond, from another corner of the world, to Haase's call to promote "genuinely comparative studies and anthologies" (*Fairy Tales and Feminism* 29).

The word *adaptations* in this book's title draws on Bacchilega's use of the term in her recent works to emphasize the intermedial nature of recent fairy-tale re-creations. This book devotes half its space to the close analysis of works of visual art inspired by fairy tales, an area that Haase also mentions as one of the important lines of inquiry to be pursued in the future but that is not explored in his volume. Although substantial studies of illustrations for fairy tales in picture books produced in different parts of the world have appeared, including Joosen's and Beckett's works mentioned above, fairy-tale intertexts in the visual arts have not yet been sufficiently examined apart from the works by such artists as Kiki Smith and Paula Rego, which have become prominent reference points in the fairy-tale web. Smith's series of works based on "Little Red Riding Hood," for example, has been frequently discussed in fairy-tale criticism,[3] used as illustrations on the front covers of both fairy-tale criticism and rewriting,[4] and reworked in other fairy-tale artworks.[5] Bacchilega's *Fairy Tales Transformed?* expands the cultural scope in this field to include a discussion of work by Chan-Hyo Bae, a Korean artist living in London, whose Existing in Costume series (2005–), she argues, can be seen as a "(de)Orientalized parody" of the "glamorizing of royalty" in European fairy tales (141).

This book covers a corpus of literary and artistic adaptations of fairy tales by Japanese women since the 1990s. The writers discussed in detail are Tawada Yōko and Ogawa Yōko, and the artists are Yanagi Miwa and Kōnoike Tomoko, all of whom were born in the 1960s. As I will argue, their works, intended chiefly for an adult audience, are engaged in complex and feminist ways with the fairy-tale traditions of both the East and the West.

These writers and artists represent two types of Japanese literature and art that began to circulate globally in the 1990s, the period following Japan's rapid economic growth throughout the 1970s and 1980s. The first type of works tends to be produced with an international audience in mind; writers and artists of this type often have an experience of living and/or working outside Japan. Tawada, for example, has long been based in Germany and writes in both Japanese and German, and Yanagi's works have received critical attention in Europe and North America from early in her career and have featured in major international art exhibitions. Often character- ized by their self-conscious reworking of the images of Japan in a global context, such works draw our attention to the cultural difference that lies beyond existing cultural stereotypes. The second type of works, represented by those of Ogawa and Kōnoike, on the other hand, is produced mainly within the cultural context of Japan, although also reaching an interna- tional audience. These works tend to focus on the transcultural aspects of fairy-tale traditions rather than emphasizing cultural dissonance, as the first type often does. By examining the uses of fairy-tale intertexts in these two types of works, I intend to show varied ways in which the fairy tale as a transcultural as well as a cross-cultural narrative tradition travels between the East and the West, highlighting the dynamics of cultural difference and continuity in today's globalizing world.

In thinking about today's global circulation of cultural products, it is important to consider the geopolitical forces operating in relationships between Western and non-Western countries. Here, it is helpful to turn to Cécile Sakai's analysis of the reception of Japanese literature in France. Sakai observes two discernible patterns of cultural transformation in the postwar French assimilation of modern Japanese literature. Some works are stripped of their Japan-specific elements to be assimilated more easily into French culture; Sakai analyzes the way in which the cultural spec- ificity of Nosaka Akiyuki's (1930–) fiction has been minimized through illustrations—drawn by a French illustrator in a conventional Oriental- ist style—and through the packaging of the DVD of the popular Studio Ghibli animation film *Hotaru no haka* (dir. Takahata Isao, 1988; Grave of the Fireflies; released in France in 1996 and based on Nosaka's 1967 semi- autobiographical novel of the same title) in order to fit into the existing Western stereotype of Japan (100). Other works, in contrast, are more readily accepted when their Japan-specific elements are emphasized or, to use Sakai's word, "staged" (101; my translation).[6] Sakai gives as examples the works of Tanizaki Jun'ichiro, Mishima Yukio, and Kawabata Yasunari, whose otherness—be it sexual perversion or minimalist aesthetics—has been foregrounded in their reception in France. "Both patterns," she claims, "have been undertaking a campaign for assimilating Japanese culture and literature into French culture and literature by transforming or deforming the otherness of Japan" (101). It is true that this kind of cultural transformation has always taken place all over the world; however, as Sakai points out, there has been and still is an imbalance in power, which is reflected in the fact that the influence of Japanese culture on Western culture has been much less significant than the influence of Western culture on the modernization of Japan. This imbalance in power between Japan and the West has a similar structure to the conflict between the Orient and the Occident analyzed by Edward Said in *Orientalism* (1978). At the same time, it is important to note that, in the process of modernization, Japan has also assumed the position of a colonizer toward other Asian countries in order to compete *and* identify with the West, an irresolvable internal conflict that, as I will argue in chapter 1, helped to give rise to the vogue for Western fairy tales in end-of-the-twentieth-century Japan.

Interestingly, Sakai also points out the gradual disappearance of cultural otherness in contemporary fiction in Japan and other parts of the world; she gives Murakami Haruki's (1949–) work as a prime example of this transcultural phenomenon. She speculates that this will ultimately lead to the redundancy of the act of translation itself since soon there will be no real otherness to be translated or transformed (101). This view certainly describes one aspect of literary globalization, that is, the shifting and blurring of linguistic and cultural boundaries currently taking place in the works of authors writing across languages and cultures (she also mentions Tawada as an example). I would argue, however, that it is also important to be aware of a more subtle yet still Orientalizing tendency at work even today, as is evident in the general preference for the bizarre and the cute in Japanese culture. This tendency, in my view, may lead to the omission of those works that re-create fairy tales in a more innovative way in favor of those that fit into cultural stereotypes such as the Ghibli films, whose main international distribution partners include the Walt Disney Corporation.

My analysis will place the works by the four Japanese women writers and artists in the context of literary criticism both in Japan and in the West while keeping in mind the persistent power imbalance at work in today's globalizing world. I will compare their works with more frequently discussed fairy-tale adaptations by Western writers and artists—above all, Angela Carter and Kiki Smith. The fairy-tale intertexts discussed here include such canonized European tales as "Snow White," "Cinderella," "Little Red Riding Hood," "Sleeping Beauty," "Beauty and the Beast," and "Bluebeard." In addition, I will also refer to less well-known European tales such as "Frau Trude" as well as Japanese fairy tales, especially animal bride and bridegroom tales and tales about a *yamauba*, or a mountain witch, as part of my attempt to provincialize the existing Western canon as defined and naturalized by such studies as Ruth B. Bottigheimer's *Fairy Tales: A New History* (2009). Before going into textual analyses, I will first give a sketch of the history of fairy-tale adaptations and scholarship in Japan since the arrival of Western fairy tales at the end of the nineteenth century in order to provide background knowledge necessary to understand the culture-specific aspects of the uses of fairy tales by the contemporary Japanese writers and artists discussed in this book.

1

the DEPTH *of* FAIRY TALES

Reclaiming Wonder for Adults

The recent vogue for European fairy tales among adults in Japan shares some characteristics with the fairy-tale renaissance in Western cultures. As in the West, the fairy tale has been liberated from the children's sphere and subjected to critical and creative reinterpretations, revealing a depth, diversity, and versatility far greater than previous generations had imagined possible. Especially notable has been the change in the role of women as (re-)creators of stories as well as the difference in the way they are represented in the genre, as women have increasingly recuperated their own voices and autonomy both in and outside stories. Furthermore, as in many Western cultures, the fairy tale has come to be regarded as a repository of hidden—often forbidden—desires, whose meanings can be traced through a psychological decoding of its symbolic language and imagery.

There are, however, some significant differences between the two phenomena. Two tendencies that seem specific to Japanese culture can be discerned, one relating to its response to European fairy tales and the other concerning its perception of Japanese tales, and both of them involve the notion of depth. The first tendency stems from the belief that beneath traditional European fairy tales lie meanings darker—more violent and more sexual—than appear on the surface. This view, although directly influenced by the Freudian interpretation of fairy tales, differs from the Western understanding in that the characters in European fairy tales often figure as the cultural Other onto whom unconscious desires, be they incestuous, murderous, or perverse, can be safely projected. The second tendency comes from the framework of Carl Jung's depth psychology modified to interpret Japanese fairy tales as narratives representing the Japanese psyche, which is assumed to be essentially different from the Western mind supposedly reflected in the Grimms' and other traditional European fairy tales. These two approaches to the fairy tale have become so prevalent in Japan that they have eclipsed some of the significant insights provided by the recent developments in fairy-tale scholarship in the West, including post-structuralist and feminist approaches.

In this chapter, after giving an overview of the history of the reception of Western fairy tales since the late nineteenth century in Japan, I will consider the development of fairy-tale production and criticism in Japan since the 1970s in comparison with the fairy-tale renaissance in the West. In doing so, I intend to illuminate some aspects of cultural continuity and cultural difference that the global circulation of fairy tales reveals to us today. I will then point to a different kind of depth of fairy tales—not necessarily sexual, violent, or archetypal—that has also been explored by contemporary fairy-tale adaptations by Japanese women writers.

TRANSLATING AND ADAPTING WESTERN FAIRY TALES

In premodern Japan, the fairy tale developed from both local storytelling traditions and Buddhist narratives from India and China. *Konjaku monogatarishū* (c. 1120; *Tales of Times Now Past*; see Ury), the most influential premodern story collection, contains both secular and religious narratives originating in Japan, China, Korea, and India.[1] In the mid-twelfth century, popular tales began to be adapted for horizontal picture scrolls, an art form combining narrative, calligraphy, and painting. These elaborate hand-painted picture scrolls circulated among the nobility and the samurai class, and those based on success stories were popular wedding gifts for brides. Another influential medieval collection is *Uji shūi monogatari* (c. 1212–21; *A Collection of Tales from Uji*; see Mills), which contains explanatory tales of a religious, courtly, and folkloric nature.

In the early seventeenth century, some of the tales began to appear in picture books accompanied by woodprint illustrations. These illustrated short stories, called *otogizōshi* (companion tales; the word *otogi* originally meant telling tales at bedtime), were often read aloud to an audience of both adults and children. About four hundred companion tales have survived, including folktales and their literary adaptations. In the 1650s, *Otogibunko* (the Companion Library), consisting of twenty-three stories accompanied by about two hundred woodprint illustrations, was published and was widely disseminated among the rising merchant class. The *Companion Library* was regarded as a source of education and entertainment especially appropriate for women and children. Some of the tales came to constitute the modern canon of fairy tales for children, such as "Urashima Tarō,"[2] a tale about a fisherman who marries a turtle princess; "Issun Bōshi" (One-Inch Boy), a tale similar to "Tom Thumb"; and "Monogusa Tarō" (Lazy Taro), a tale about a country boy who becomes rich by his wits, as well as now less well-known tales such as "Hachikazuki" (The Bowl Girl; figure 1.1), a tale similar to "Cinderella" and "The Donkey Skin" in which the heroine, bearing a large bowl on her head, flees from her evil stepmother and, after working as a housemaid at a nobleman's house, marries his youngest son.

Translations of Western fairy tales began just after the Meiji Restoration in 1868, which marked the end of a period of national seclusion lasting more than two hundred years. In 1873, the first Japanese translation of tales by the Grimms and Hans Christian Andersen, translated from *Sargent's Standard Third Reader,* an English textbook published in America in 1857, appeared in a collection of stories for children's moral education titled *Keimō shūshin roku* (Readings on Enlightenment and

FIGURE 1.1. "Hachikazuki" (The Bowl Girl). Illustrator unknown. *Sanzōshi emaki,* n.d. The Digitized Contents of the National Diet Library.

Morals) (Fukawa 141–50) . From then on, Western fairy tales, especially those by the Grimms, appeared in various translations and adaptations in teaching materials at primary schools practicing the educational method advocated at the beginning of the nineteenth century by Johann Friedrich Herbart, a German philosopher and founder of pedagogy as an academic discipline. On the one hand, Herbart's systematic educational method was welcomed by Japanese educators at a time when Japan was eager to catch up with the modernity of the West. On the other hand, Herbart's theory was in accord with the country's sense of rising nationalism, spurred by apprehensions about losing national identity in the process of modernization; as Nagura Yōko argues, Herbart's key concepts were mapped onto Confucian ideas and made suitable for nationalistic moral education emphasizing feudal values.[3]

The first actual collection of the Grimms' tales in Japanese, however, was intended mainly for adult readers. In 1887, Suga Ryōhō published *Seiyō koji: Shinsen sōwa* (Western Folklore: A Collection of Supernatural Tales), which contained eleven stories from the Grimms' collection, including "Cinderella" and "Faithful John." Although no source is shown—not even the names of the Brothers Grimm are mentioned—Noguchi Yoshiko ("Eiyakubon kara jūyaku sareta nihon no Gurimu dōwa") infers from the stylistic and editorial characteristics that Suga used Mrs. H. B. Paull's English translation (1868), in which Paull removed some violent and sexual expressions she considered inappropriate for Victorian readers. As the expression "Supernatural Tales" in the subtitle suggests, Suga's translation underlines the magical and exotic aspects of the tales, which is a tendency also evident in the title of each story: "Cinderella," for example, is rendered as "The Strange Fate of Cinderella."

This emphasis on the exotic in old stories seems to derive from the oral tradition of otogi, whose main audience was adults. Suga, a Buddhist monk who studied philosophy at Oxford University and later became a politician, wrote in a sophisticated literary style, not only introducing new expressions to describe Western social and cultural customs but also adding moral messages suitable for the dominant feudalistic and Confucian ideas of his time. In "The Strange Fate of Cinderella," for example, the king, only a very marginal figure in the Grimms' tale, is portrayed as a ruler of great moral integrity worthy of the loyalty of his subjects; the virtue of diligence is even more emphasized than in the original; and devotion to one's parents becomes the most important lesson of the story. In translating the Grimms' tales, Suga thus both exoticized and domesticated them for a Japanese adult readership.

The first tale translated from Perrault's 1697 collection was "Cinderella," which appeared in 1886 in a newspaper run by Yano Ryūkei, a government official and a civil rights activist eager to import modern Western constitutionalism. Yano also wrote a foreword to the first substantial collection of French fairy tales, the 1896 *Seiyō senkyō kidan* (de Beaumont et al.; Strange Stories of Fairy Land in the West), whose title, like that of Suga's collection, emphasizes the exotic aspect of the tales. The work includes abbreviated versions of five stories by Perrault, four by Madame de Beaumont, two by the Countess de Murat, and one by Madame de Villeneuve, all of which are translated by Inoue Kan'ichi apparently from an English text (the English titles are given as "the original titles"). The stated aim of this collection is to promote Japan's modernization by introducing popular fairy tales, which Yano believes constitute the foundation of Western mentality. The stories are largely Japanized so that readers can familiarize themselves with "strange" Western culture more readily. For

FIGURE 1.2. Illustration for "Aohige" (Bluebeard). Yamamoto Shōun. *Seiyō senkyō kidan*, by Jeanne-Marie Leprince de Beaumont et al. and translated by Inoue Kan'ichi. Tokyo: Tōyōdō, 1896. The Digitized Contents of the National Diet Library. Courtesy of Yamamoto Haruko.

example, Perrault's "Bluebeard," as the illustration indicates (figure 1.2), is interpreted as a story assimilable to the literary and artistic tradition of Japanese ghost stories and is rendered more gory than Perrault's original and the later Victorian versions.

In the 1890s, Iwaya Sazanami (1870–1933), often considered the pioneer of children's literature in Japan, began to translate the Grimms' tales from the German for children's magazines; it was Iwaya who first used the term *otogibanashi* (*banashi* meaning a tale) to refer to Western fairy tales such as the Grimms' and Andersen's as well as traditional Japanese otogizōshi and played a leading role in establishing a new genre of literary fairy tales intended specifically for children. Iwaya promoted the use of fairy tales not so much for children's moral education as for their entertainment, and the stories' enthusiastic reception brought about a vogue for literary fairy tales for children in the 1890s.

Iwaya's translations of Western tales, which were the most widely read versions at the time and which had a significant impact on subsequent translations of fairy tales, are more adaptations than translations. In his "Koyukihime" (1896; Snow White), for example, not only is the whole setting, including characters, places, and customs, transported to Japan, as the illustration makes clear (figure 1.3), but also some major structural elements of the story are altered: the prince, for example, makes no appearance at all throughout the story while the wicked stepmother receives no punishment other than mild ridicule for her vanity at the abrupt ending of the story when, after breaking the magic mirror in a rage, she asks herself who the most beautiful woman in the world is and answers that it is herself. Iwaya's fairy tales are generally imbued with this kind of playful irony, which later came to be regarded as unsuitable for a child readership.

Iwaya not only published a large number of translations and adaptations of fairy tales from around the world in magazines and anthologies for children, he also wrote stories for children himself, such as *Koganemaru* (1891; Golden Boy), and founded an influential children's magazine, *Shōnen sekai* (1895–c. 1933; The Boy's World). At the turn of the twentieth century, fairy-tale collections and other books intended for a child readership became popular Christmas gifts among Japanese upper-class families as more people began to adopt Western customs in everyday life. Iwaya's role in institutionalizing the fairy tale for children may be

少女

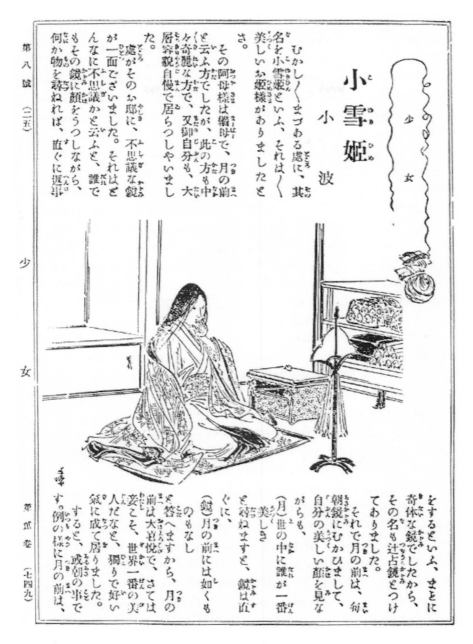

小雪姫

小波

少女

むかし／＼まづある處に、其名を小雪姫といふ、それはく美しいお姫様がありましたとさ。

その阿母様は繼母で、月の前と云ふ方でしたが、此の方も々奇麗な方で、又御自分も、大厨容貌自慢で居らつしやいました。

處がそのお邸に、不思議な鏡が一面でございました。それはどんなに不思議かと云ふと、誰でもその鏡に顔をうつしながら、何か物を尋ねれば、直ぐに返事

をするといふ、まさに奇体な鏡でしたから、その名も辻占鏡とつけてありました。

それで月の前は、毎「朝鏡にひかひまして、自分の美しい顔を見ながらも、

（月）世の中に誰が一番美しき

と尋ねますと、鏡は直ぐに、

（鏡）月の前には如くものもなし

と答へますから、月の前は大岩悦で、さては姿こそ、世界一番の美人だなど、獨りで好い氣に成て居りました。

すると、或朝の事で例の様に月の前は、

FIGURE 1.3. "Koyukihime" (Snow White), by Jacob and Wilhelm Grimm and translated by Iwaya Sazanami. Illustrator unknown. *Shōnen sekai*, 1896. Courtesy of Hakubunkan Shinsha.

comparable to the role played by Andrew Lang in the history of English-language children's literature, allowing many children to enjoy traditional tales from different cultures in an accessible form.

Despite his own claim to the contrary, however, Iwaya's stories, either translated or created, are imbued with the same old feudalistic values endorsed in teaching materials for moral education. He later became an advocate for a nationalist educational policy that he called Momotarōism after the popular fairy tale "Momotarō" (Peach Boy), in which a boy born of a peach sets out on an expedition to subjugate ogres living in a faraway island.[4] "Momotarō" came to be widely used as imperialistic propaganda during the series of international wars in which Japan was involved until the end of the Second World War, and it still remains one of the best-known fairy tales in Japan. Japan's wartime use of the fairy-tale symbolism of good and evil, which the historian John Dower calls the Momotaro paradigm,[5] has been criticized from postcolonialist perspectives. (I will come back to this point in my discussion of Tawada Yōko's work in chapter 2.)

In the early twentieth century, the rigorous method of the Herbart school gradually began to be replaced by a more liberal theory of education allowing children more freedom and independence. The Grimms' and other European fairy tales, now reinterpreted within the framework of European romanticism, came to be incorporated into a newly defined genre of children's literature represented by *Akai tori* (Red Bird), a children's magazine established by Suzuki Miekichi in 1918. With this redefinition of children's literature, the fairy tale was renamed *dōwa* (children's stories), severing the genre from otogi, the storytelling tradition for adults' entertainment, whose trace could still be found in Iwaya's retellings, as Kawahara Kazue observes (61–62). Although the *Red Bird* approach to fairy tales puts more emphasis on aesthetic and creative values than on moral and regulatory functions, it is nevertheless as emphatically educational and censorious as the previous approach; its editorial policy is to remove elements unsuitable for the romanticized notion of *dōshin* (children's minds), conceived to be fundamentally different from the impure minds of adults. Although the magazine's dōshin-ism was later criticized as too abstract and elitist, many story collections for children published since then have followed its approach to some extent, and the expurgation of what adults regarded as too immoral or ugly for children in fairy tales continued throughout the twentieth century.

However, an attempt to bridge the gap between the educational and folkloristic approaches to the Grimms' tales began to appear in the 1920s. Kaneda Kiichi (1886–1963), a scholar and translator of German literature, published the first complete translation of *Die Kinder-und Hausmärchen* in two volumes in 1924 and 1927 as a part of *Sekai dōwa taikei* (An Anthology of World Children's Literature). Kaneda translated 248 tales altogether: not only all 211 tales in the seventh edition of the Grimms' work (1857) but also 22 tales that the Grimms excluded after the first edition, 9 posthumous tales, and 6 fragments. Kaneda's intention was to translate the Grimms' tales in such a way that both children and adults could enjoy them. He rejected the commonly held view of the time that adults had the right to censor literature for children, stating in the introduction that "it is truly lamentable that adults are gradually damaging children's pure minds with the almost demonic goodwill arising from their conscious and unconscious sense of privilege" (7). His translation, therefore, makes no attempt to remove or alter the violent and sexual elements previously regarded as unsuitable for children. His unabridged and faithful translation of the Grimms' collection was influenced by the rise of scholarship on children's literature that began to incorporate a folkloristic perspective in the 1910s (Nagura 138–41). It can be said, however, that Kaneda's translation has been mainly appreciated for its scholarly and literary value.

In the early twentieth century, some writers began to turn to the Western fairy tale as a medium for exploring new forms of expression in modern literature for adults. Izumi Kyōka's (1873–1939) romantic reworking of supernatural motifs in folklore from the East and the West is said to have had a formative influence on modern fantasy literature in Japan. His best-known work, "Kōya hijiri" (1900; "The Holy Man of Mount Kōya"), for example, tells the story of a young Buddhist monk's encounter with a Circe-like enchantress who transforms her victims into repugnant creatures such as snakes, frogs, and leeches. Tanizaki Jun'ichirō's (1886–1965) "Ningyo no nageki" (1917; The Mermaid's Lament) rewrites Andersen's "The Little Mermaid" as a decadent story about a rich man who buys a Western mermaid as a curio. Tanizaki's story is written in an ornate style influenced by Oscar Wilde's aesthetics and accompanies illustrations evocative of Aubrey Beardsley's sensual Orientalist images. Both Izumi's and Tanizaki's interest in fairy tales was stimulated by the partial translation of French and English translations of the *Arabian Nights*, which began to appear in 1875.[6] The Nobel laureate Kawabata Yasunari's *Nemureru bijo* (1961; Sleeping Beauty; translated into English as *House of the Sleeping Beauties* in 1969) follows this tradition of using fairy-tale motifs to evoke gothic and erotic images and atmosphere. Kawabata's novella tells the story of an aging man who frequents a brothel where customers pay to spend a night with young girls narcotized into unconsciousness.[7] It can be said that these early fairy-tale retellings for adult readers use Western fairy tales as a source of exotic eroticism and are largely uncritical of the conventions and ideologies of the genre, as is evident in their mystification and victimization of women. It was not until the 1970s that Japanese writers and artists began to revisit fairy tales of both Asian and European traditions for revisioning purposes.

DISCOVERING THE DEPTH OF FAIRY TALES: THE 1970s AND 1980s

In 1970, Shibusawa Tatsuhiko (1928–87) began to publish his translation of Perrault's stories in serial form in *an-an*, a newly founded magazine targeted at young women who were keen to explore the emerging possibilities of their financial, emotional, and sexual independence resulting from the rapid economic growth and the Americanization of postwar Japan. Its intended readership, therefore, had some similarities with Perrault's upper-class female audiences in the age of the Enlightenment, who had strong social and intellectual ambitions. Shibusawa's translations of Perrault's tales were collected and published with illustrations by Katayama Ken in 1973. Katayama's illustrations (figure 1.4) underline the surrealistic and erotic overtones in Shibusawa's rendering.

Shibusawa, scholar of French literature, writer, and translator, was heavily influenced by the works of European avant-garde writers and artists such as Georges Bataille and Hans Bellmer and was seen as a literary enfant terrible at the time, especially after being charged with obscenity for his 1959 abridged translation of the Marquis de Sade's *Juliette* (1797–1801). In his collection of essays *Erotishizumu* (1967; Eroticism), Shibusawa points out the sexual implications of European fairy tales

FIGURE 1.4. Illustration for "Akazukin-chan" (Little Red Riding Hood), by Katayama Ken. *Nagagutsu o haita neko* (Puss in Boots), by Charles Perrault and translated by Shibusawa Tatsuhiko. Tokyo: Daiwa Shobō, 1973. 26–27. Courtesy of Daiwa Shobō.

by quoting the psychoanalytic interpretations of Marie Bonaparte and Erich Fromm, heralding the psychoanalytically oriented interpretation of fairy tales that became popular in Japan at the end of the twentieth century. However, his references to psychoanalytic ideas, such as Bonaparte's interpretation of the spindle in "Sleeping Beauty" as a symbol of the girl's clitoris and Erich Fromm's interpretation of the color red in "Little Red Riding Hood" as a symbol of blood flowing through defloration, do not seem to be intended to help the reader's understanding of the complex psychological implications of these tales but only to arouse his or her erotic curiosity.

Shibusawa's translation, criticism, and rewriting of fairy tales have certainly influenced subsequent fairy-tale re-creations in both literature and art; however, his work relating to the fairy tale did not itself give rise to a widespread vogue for fairy tales among adults. One reason seems to be that his work belongs to the kind of intellectual elitism that does not examine its chauvinistic assumptions, thereby failing to respond to the changing ideas about women's subjectivity and sexuality. In *Eroticism*, for example, he denounces feminists' demystification of female virginity—his characterization of Simone de Beauvoir as "a progressive intellectual desperate to achieve women's freedom and independence" is clearly intended as a sneer in the context of this essay (112)—and reasserts the classic twin images of women as objects of male desire: "A virgin can satisfy the psychological erotic desire which a whore cannot satisfy" (114). He sanctifies the condition of a virginal girl as "the most erotic existence": she is "closest to an object or a thing because she is unable to speak and is totally passive," a state that, he claims, does not apply to a male virgin (118). Although women writers and artists have also been influenced by Shibusawa's reinterpretation of fairy tales as symbolic expressions of latent desires, their own female-centered recastings, as I will argue below, both consciously and unconsciously challenge his phallocentric view of sexuality and desire.[8] In particular, Kōnoike's illustrations for his retelling of an old Japanese story about a fox enchantress will be discussed in chapter 5.

In women's writings during the 1970s, the folkloric figure of a yamauba, often translated as a "mountain witch" (*yama* meaning "a mountain," and *uba* "an old woman" or "a crone"),[9] began to emerge as a recurring topos. In 1971, Baba Akiko (1928–), a poet specializing in *tanka* (a classical Japanese verse form consisting of thirty-one syllables) and critic, published *Oni no kenkyū* (Studies on Demons). Baba's analysis of demons—especially female demons, including the yamauba—in Japanese folklore, medieval literature, and Noh drama revealed for the first time the possibility of understanding female demons as an embodiment of marginalized femininity in a male-dominated society. Her book of poetry *Hikashō* (1972; Flying Flower Poems, included in *Baba Akiko kashū* in 1978) includes several poems written from a demon's point of view: "I am a demon. / With a stigma on my body, I sometimes cry out, wanting to sprout" (14). Her radical reinterpretation of premodern representations of demons as social dissidents who choose to transform themselves into nonhuman beings, a theme in sympathy with the emerging feminist and other antiestablishment movements at the time, still continues to inspire literary, artistic, and dramatic re-creations of this powerful female figure. Literary reworkings of the yamauba that appeared in the 1970s include Ōba Minako's "Yamauba no bishō" (1976; translated into English as "The Smile of the Mountain Witch" in 1991) and Tsushima Yūko's *Chōji* (1978; translated into English as *Child of Fortune* in 1983). These critical and creative works on folkloric motifs produced in the 1970s tend to focus on female victimhood in a patriarchal society and depict mature women who struggle in vain to break free from conventional notions of femininity and motherhood.[10]

It was also in the 1970s that Kawai Hayao (1928–2007), a psychologist trained at the Jung Institute in Zurich in the 1960s, began to publish his analysis of fairy tales from the perspective of Jungian depth psychology. His 1977 *Mukashibanashi no shinsō: Yungu shinrigaku to Gurimu dōwa* (Depth of Folktales: Jungian Psychology and the Grimms' Tales) draws both on Marie von Franz's Jungian interpretation of fairy tales and on the work of the folklorist Seki Keigo (1899–1990), who classified Japanese folktales according to the system used in Antti Aarne and Stith Thompson's *The Types of the Folktale* (1928) and who heralded a comparative analysis of Japanese tales in an international context. Kawai's *Depth of Folktales* has widely popularized the archetypal interpretation of fairy tales, which has become more influential in Japan than the Freudian approach represented by such works as Bruno Bettelheim's *The Uses of Enchantment: The Meaning and Importance of Fairy Tales* (1976; Japanese translation 1978).

In 1979, the folklorist Ozawa Toshio (1930–) published *Sekai no minwa: Hito to dōbutsu tono kon'intan* (Folktales around the World: Tales of Marriage between Humans and Animals). Ozawa's analysis of the animal bridegroom tale integrates Seki's and Kawai's comparative perspectives with Max Lüthi's stylistic approach in *The European Folktale: Form and Nature* (1947), which Ozawa translated into Japanese in 1969. Ozawa's critical works, translations, editorial works, and promotion of oral storytelling have had a significant impact on the general understanding of both international and domestic folktales in Japan, cultivating an intellectual interest in the genre among adult readers and helping to change the commonly accepted view of the fairy tale as a genre specifically for children.

The 1980s saw a rise in the wider public interest in the uses of traditional fairy tales for understanding the psychological problems of contemporary society. In 1982, the abridged translation of the American journalist Colette Dowling's *Cinderella Complex: Women's Hidden Fear of Independence* (1981) was published to wide public acclaim. The phrase "Cinderella complex," however, was stripped of its feminist implications and gained general currency in Japanese as a descriptive—and often derogatory—term for vain young women who cannot marry because of their unrealistic expectations for their marriage partners. This distortion seems to stem from an implicit and explicit social disapproval of an increasing number of young women who began to enjoy a new social status as a *kyariaūman* (career woman), a Japanese term for a woman who chooses to pursue a career rather than becoming a housewife, which at the time meant remaining single as it was still customary for women to give up their jobs and "enter the home" after marriage. (The term *kyariaūman* has now become obsolete because of its sexist implications.) The Cinderella complex phenomenon in the 1980s, therefore, did not encourage a feminist approach that sees traditional fairy tales as a reflection of social and psychological forces inhibiting women's independence, or as a cultural construct that can be reworked in order to explore alternative ways of thinking and living.

In the same year as the term *Cinderella complex* attracted wide public attention, Kawai's *Mukashibanashi to nihonjin no kokoro* (translated into English as *The Japanese Psyche: Major Motifs in the Fairy Tales of Japan* in 1988) was published to wide critical and public acclaim. Kawai states in the introduction that this work stemmed from his questioning of the universal validity of the Jungian scheme in analyzing traditional Japanese fairy tales, which he saw as having a deep structure fundamentally different from that of Western fairy tales. He combines Jung's models with concepts in Japanese culture such as *mu* (nothingness), *aware* (sorrowful beauty), and *urami* (resentment) in order to explicate the cultural specificity of the Japanese psyche reflected in fairy tales. Through his comparative analysis of Japanese tales in relation to their Western counterparts, mainly those in the Grimms' collection, Kawai comes to the conclusion that the Japanese psyche is represented by the female figure in the fairy tale whereas Western tales are structured by masculine principles. His book, therefore, is organized around various female characters—mountain witches, nonhuman brides, daughters who endure, wives who do not eat, women of will, and so on—who are seen as reflecting different aspects of the ego, whether male or female.

This predominance of feminine archetypes, however, can in turn be interpreted as a projection of Kawai's own anima—the Jungian term for the feminine part of a man's personality—onto Japanese fairy tales, a projection that again works to typecast women, albeit in a different framework. As Watanabe Manabu points out, Kawai's apparently deliberate avoidance of the term *anima* in his analysis of Japanese folktales seems to support this view (331). Although Kawai claims that the Jungian notions of masculine and feminine archetypes, or animus and anima, are not the same as men and women in real life, they nevertheless tend to collapse into the anatomical categories of sex, especially through his persistent emphasis on metaphors of the womb, women's procreative potential, and their maternal instinct. Equally problematic is the way in which his generalization of the contrast between the Japanese psyche and the Western psyche works to reinforce the typecasting of the East-West opposition as unconscious versus conscious, which is mapped onto the opposition between feminine and masculine.

As some of Angela Carter's fairy-tale retellings in *The Bloody Chamber* were "the result of quarrelling furiously with Bettelheim" (Haffenden 83), this study is partly motivated by my arguments with Kawai's modified Jungian model. One of my chief objectives is to reconsider Kawai's analytical framework from the perspective of post-structuralist feminist fairy-tale criticism and to offer an alternative to its sexually and culturally essentialistic approach to fairy tales while nevertheless incorporating its valuable insights. Kawai's theory has been influential in the general understanding of fairy tales in Japan not only because of its focus on Japanese material but also because of its comparative approach, which pays attention to the international variants of a particular tale or a motif, an approach that I also adopt in my cross-cultural analysis of fairy-tale intertexts in contemporary Japanese literature and art.

The 1980s were also important in the development of Grimm scholarship in Japan. Coinciding with Jacob Grimm's bicentenary anniversary in 1985, translations of the older editions of the Grimms' collection as well as a series of substantial critical works on their tales by Japanese scholars began to appear. Especially influential was the publication in 1985 of *Gendai ni ikiru Gurimu* (Ozawa et al.; The Grimms Still Living Today), a collection of scholarly essays from philological, linguistic, historical, folkloristic, literary, and psychological (Jungian) perspectives by five Japanese scholars, including Ozawa and Kawai, together with Ozawa's translation of Heinz Rölleke's seminal essay "The 'Utterly Hessian' Fairy Tales by 'Old Marie': The End of a Myth" (1974).

The gender bias of this otherwise innovatively interdisciplinary collection is evident from the fact that none of its contributors—not surprisingly, all male—engages with the significant insights afforded by a substantial body of feminist reinterpretations of the Grimms' tales by Western scholars such as Jack Zipes, Maria Tatar, and Ruth Bottigheimer, which had appeared before 1985. Moreover, despite the fact that the Grimm specialist Noguchi Yoshiko had first introduced Rölleke's aforementioned essay in a Japanese journal as early as in 1977, her article had been ignored and was not even mentioned in the book. Nor did Noguchi's subsequent critical works on the Grimms' tales from a feminist perspective receive wide attention until much later; her collection of essays since the late 1970s, *Gurimu no meruhyen: Sono yume to genjitsu* (Grimm's Märchen: Dream and Reality), was finally published in 1994.[11] The main thrust of Noguchi's argument is to reveal the gender bias underlying the Grimms' collection as a reflection of the social and religious ideologies current at the time, emphasizing the way in which the tales stereotype young women as passive victims and older women as evil stepmothers and witches. As we will see later, it was not until the 1990s that a more female-centered approach to the fairy tale became widespread in Japan, and it took a different form from that in the West.

WOMEN'S FAIRY-TALE RETELLINGS: THE 1980s

A work often regarded as the equivalent of Carter's feminist fairy-tale rewriting in Japan was published by Kurahashi Yumiko in 1984, a year before Jacob Grimm's bicentenary. Kurahashi's *Otona no tame no zankoku dōwa* (Cruel Fairy Tales for Adults) is a collection of twenty-six stories based on fairy tales, myths, and literary texts from around the world. Its association with Carter's *The Bloody Chamber* in the Japanese context is made clear in the subtitle of the Japanese translation in 1992 of Carter's collection, *Chizome no heya: Otona no tame no gensō dōwa* (The Bloody Chamber: Fantastic Fairy Tales for Adults), echoing Kurahashi's *Cruel Fairy Tales for Adults*.[12] That Carter would not have liked the word *adults* in the Japanese title is clear from the comment that she made on the 1981 American edition of her collection, titled *The Bloody Chamber and Other Adult Tales:* "My intention was not to do 'versions' or, as the American edition of the book said, horribly, 'adult' fairy tales, but to extract the latent content from the traditional stories and to use it as the beginnings of new stories" (Haffenden 80).

Despite the words *cruel* and *adult* in the title, however, Kurahashi's collection is not primarily an attempt to sensationalize the violent and sexual aspects of fairy tales. Her fairy-tale retelling is informed more by the postmodern stylistic literary experiments evident in such works as Donald Barthelme's *Snow White* (1967; Japanese translation in 1995) and Robert Coover's *Pricksongs and Descants* (1969) than by the feminist and sociocultural fairy-tale scholarship and fairy-tale rewritings that began to appear in the West in the 1970s. Kurahashi's stories certainly contain elements of the postmodern reconfiguration of sexual politics found in Carter's fairy-tale rewriting, but her primary concern is neither feminist nor folkloric, and her playful irony and black humor are directed at the absurdities of people, men and women alike, adhering to gender and other cultural stereotypes. In her "Snow White," for example, the prince decides to marry the wicked queen, who is more sexually attractive and intelligent than her pretty but dull stepdaughter. After making the prince murder the aging king, the queen smashes the mirror and says smilingly: "I've done away with an evil spirit that had been haunting me for a long time" (36), an episode echoing the ironic humor of Iwaya's "Snow White" mentioned earlier. Meanwhile, we are told that Snow White, although her beauty had been impaired by her stepmother, lived "fairly" happily ever after with the seven dwarves, bearing numerous little babies for them. The moral of Kurahashi's "Snow White" can be read only ironically: "Fools will never be happy" (37).

The word *cruel* in the title of Kurahashi's collection refers to the cruelty resulting from what she calls the "rationalism" of fairy tales. In the afterword to her book, Kurahashi explains what she means by "cruel fairy tales":

> [T]he world of fairy tales possesses a coherent law and logic. This system of law and logic constitutes magic, and magic creates the supernatural world in an orderly and logical manner. That is why the supernatural world of fairy tales is filled with rationalism. The fairy-tale style is precise and lucid, with no unnecessary descriptions of psychology and nature, and the world proceeds in an orderly fashion. Neither sympathy nor sentimentality can change the consequences of this rational process. It is in this sense that the world of fairy tales is cruel. (223)

The unrelenting rationalism of her fairy-tale universe spares no one, and its bleak worldview leaves no room for a happy ending except in an ironic way. Kurahashi's tales overturn the conventional idea of good and evil by following the logic of the fairy-tale universe until it lends itself to the opposite of what it purports to prescribe. In doing so, these tales also undercut the culturally conditioned premises underlying traditional fairy tales. The cruel rationalism of her tales can be compared to what Carter calls "the politics of experience" in Perrault's tales: "Charles Perrault . . . takes a healthily abrasive attitude to his material. Cut the crap about richly nurturing the imagination. *This* world is all that is to the point" ("The Better to Eat You With" 452–53). As Martine Hennard Dutheil de la Rochère argues in "Updating the Politics of Experience: Angela Carter's Translation of Charles Perrault's 'Le petit chaperon rouge,'" it is in this spirit of a rationalist that Carter rewrites fairy tales in *The Bloody Chamber.*

Kurahashi's *Cruel Fairy Tales for Adults* attracted wide critical and general attention and helped arouse the interest of adult audiences in the literary reworking of traditional fairy tales; however, it also served to obscure the feminist impulse in the modern fairy-tale rewriting in the West represented by Carter's collection. As Luciana Cardi points out in her analysis of Kurahashi's retelling of "Snow White," Kurahashi's views about women's role largely conformed to the conservative ideology of the time (196–97).

FIGURE 1.5. Illustration for "Shirayukihime" (Snow White), by Sano Yōko. ©JIROCHO, Inc. *Uso bakka: Shinshaku sekai otogibanashi,* by Sano Yōko. 1985. Tokyo: Kōdansha, 1998. 41. Courtesy of JIROCHO, Inc.

In 1985, writer and lithographer Sano Yōko published *Uso bakka: Shinshaku sekai otogibanashi* (All Lies: New Interpretations of Fairy Tales from around the World), a collection of twenty-six stories based on tales by the Grimms, Andersen, and Aesop as well as Japanese fairy tales. While Kurahashi's collection shows a close affinity with the Sadeian aspect of Carter's work in her fairy-tale retellings such as "The Bloody Chamber" and "The Snow Child" as well as in her novels, most notably *The Infernal Desire Machines of Doctor Hoffmann* (1972), Sano's collection can be associated with Carter's carnivalesque side, most evident in her rewriting of "Puss-in-Boots" and in her later novels such as *Nights at the Circus* (1984) and *Wise Children* (1991). Sano's fairy-tale rewriting is characterized by its succinct and fluid style and its ironic yet hearty humor, which is also evident in her own illustrations for her stories (figure 1.5). Although apparently not theoretically informed, Sano's reworking overturns various hierarchical dichotomies in fairy tales such as good versus evil, beauty versus ugliness, wisdom versus folly, and male versus female through unexpected maneuvers, offering alternative ways of embracing the richness and complexity of life.

Sano's retelling of "Snow White," for example, reappropriates the mirror for women by restoring its ability to reflect the beauty of the world as it is, undistorted by human—predominantly male—prejudices. The story is told from the perspective of the wicked queen, who laments her own unsurpassable beauty: "I have nothing more beautiful than myself in the world" (42). She envies her stepdaughter not because of her youthful beauty—Snow White, on the contrary, has an extremely ugly appearance in this story—but because of her ability to take pleasure in the beauty of the world of nature. In this retelling, the magic mirror, the crucial motif in "Snow White," is internalized by the girl, who can enjoy the beauty of nature as it presents itself in forms such as the bright colors of a caterpillar—a reference to the heroine of the twelfth-century Japanese tale "Mushi mezuru himegimi" (The Lady Who Loved Insects), who defies the conventional notion of feminine beauty and decorum[13]—and the different shades of darkness in stormy clouds. On her way back from the dwarves' cabin, the queen feels miserable and envies her ugly but happy stepdaughter. The queen, however, is not without hope since she is now at least aware of another kind of mirror other than her old one which, as Sandra M. Gilbert and Susan Gubar point out in *The Mad Woman in the Attic: The Woman Writer and the Nineteenth-Century Literary Imagination* (1979),[14] represents the patriarchal gaze and works to set different generations of women against each other.

Importantly, the older woman is not always cast as evil in Sano's stories. Her retelling of "Cinderella" is told from the perspective of the innocent stepmother who falls victim to a marriage plot elaborated by her beautiful and overambitious stepdaughter. Here, Cinderella devises a stratagem to attract people's sympathy by performing the role of an innocent girl forced to live among the ashes by her evil stepmother and two stepsisters, who are less physically attractive—and therefore less convincing—than she herself is in the eyes of the curious masses of the kingdom. After she succeeds in marrying the prince, the kitchen stove to which she claims she used to be consigned by her evil stepmother becomes a popular tourist attraction among her people, to whom she appears a beautiful and benevolent queen. Although neither explicitly nor primarily feminist in its purpose, Sano's adaptation humorously subverts the conflation of external attractiveness and inner virtues in female characters in such traditional tales as "Cinderella" and caricatures the contemporary society in which women's lives are often determined by their physical appearances through the images proliferated by mass media. Unlike Kurahashi's popular collection published a year before, however, Sano's collection attracted little attention compared to her other works, as the author herself complains in the afterword to its third edition, published in 1998. This relative neglect may be partly due to her style which, unlike Kurahashi's tone, imbued with aesthetics drawn from Shibusawa's work, treats the elements of sex and violence with open and life-affirming humor.[15]

SEX, VIOLENCE, AND THE GRIMM BOOM: THE 1990s

Translator and cultural critic Suzuki Shō's 1991 paperback volume *Gurimu dōwa: Meruhen no shinsō* (Grimms' Tales: Depth of Märchen) was one of the most widely read books that introduced the new critical approaches to the fairy tale in the West to general Japanese readers. Suzuki's introductory book draws mainly on works by Tatar, Bottigheimer, and Zipes, some of which he also translated: his translations of Tatar's 1987 *The Hard Facts of the Grimms' Fairy Tales* and Bottigheimer's 1987 *Grimms' Bad Girls and Bold Boys* both came out in 1990, followed by his translation of Zipes's 1988 *The Brothers Grimm: From Enchanted Forests to the Modern World* in 1991. The emphasis of Suzuki's introductory book falls on the sexual and violent aspects of the Grimms' tales revealed by Freudian interpretations such as those given by Tatar's *The Hard Facts of the Grimms' Fairy Tales.* The word *depth* in the subtitle, therefore, is related more closely to Freud's theory of the unconscious and infantile sexuality than to the desexualized notion of the collective unconscious in Jungian-Kawaian psychology. Suzuki's book opens with a chapter revealing the cruel elements in the Grimms' tales that have been suppressed in their modern translations and adaptations, such as those found in "How Some Children Played at Slaughtering," a tale omitted after the first edition, and "Snow White," a tale circulated in a heavily sanitized version. Despite his knowledge of the latest feminist fairy-tale criticism in the West, however, Suzuki does not discuss any of the key rewriters, such as Angela Carter and Margaret Atwood, who have had a decisive influence on the development of feminist fairy-tale criticism in English-language culture. Apart from

Diana Coles's *The Clever Princess* (1983; Japanese translation in 1989), which he regards as one of the few successful examples of a feminist fairy tale, Suzuki sweepingly dismisses the whole genre of feminist fairy-tale rewriting as uninteresting. Despite this blind spot, Suzuki's introductory book on the "depth" of the Grimms' tales, which sold more than ten thousand copies in the 1990s, together with his translations of some of the key English-language criticism, paved the way for the subsequent rise of fairy-tale adaptations written mainly by women writers.

The final two years of the twentieth century saw a remarkable vogue for fairy-tale rewritings and anthologies for adult readers, a phenomenon often referred to as the *Gurimu būmu* (Grimm boom). The work that heralded the Grimm boom was Matsumoto Yūko's rewriting of the Grimms' and Andersen's tales, collected under the title *Tsumibukai hime no otogibanashi* (1996; Fairy Tales of Sinful Princesses) and illustrated by Higami Kumiko. The combination of Matsumoto's female-oriented fairy tales and Higami's sensual portraits of princesses set a vogue for illustrated fairy-tale collections for adults, especially those addressing a female readership. In an intertextual manner characteristic of the Grimm boom, Matsumoto indicates in the moral at the end of each tale and in her afterword that her stories are based on the older editions of the Grimms' tales and are informed by the recent fairy-tale criticism of Tatar, Zipes, Bottigheimer, Alan Dundes (his 1988 *Cinderella: A Casebook* was translated into Japanese in 1991), and other Western scholars, an approach that echoes the late twentieth-century trend of blurred boundaries between fairy-tale retellings and fairy-tale criticism in Europe and North America as delineated in Joosen's *Critical and Creative Perspectives on Fairy Tales*.

Matsumoto's rewriting of "Cinderella," titled "Shinderera to ōashi no anetachi" (Cinderella and Her Big-Footed Sisters), for example, combines the most widely known version by Perrault with the motifs and episodes found in the Grimms' and other less well-known versions of the tale, such as the hazel twig that the heroine plants on her mother's grave in the Grimms' version and her shoes made of fur, a reference to the disputed idea that Perrault changed the material of her shoes from *vair* (fur) to *verre* (glass) in his retelling. More innovative is her incorporation of feminist fairy-tale criticism. In her version of "Cinderella," she criticizes the idealization of women's small feet as a symbol of feminine virtues and explicitly associates the heroine's unusually small feet with the misogynistic custom of foot binding in China; the prince, inflamed with a fetishistic passion for her feet, forces her to wear tiny glass high heels all the time, which gradually deform her whole body. As the author and illustrator themselves acknowledge, both Matsumoto's rewritings and Higami's pictures, like most of the subsequent Grimm boom works by others, are deeply influenced by Shibusawa's work, enhancing the erotic implications of fairy tales so as to entertain adult readers even while expressing their female-centered concerns.

Then in 1998, a collection of sensationalized retellings of the Grimms' tales by Kiryū Misao, titled *Hontō wa osoroshii Gurimu dōwa* (Grimms' Tales Really Are Horrific), was published. It, together with its sequel in 1999, sold more than 2.5 million copies. This huge commercial success led to the publication of numerous books with similar titles emphasizing the cruel and sexual aspects not only of the Grimms' tales but also of folk and fairy tales from around the world. Because of its misleading title, Kiryū's collection has spread the faulty impression that these "horrific" rewritings, rather than being creative embellishments, are the "real" versions of the Grimm tales.[16] Although the Grimm boom lasted for only about two years, this vogue radically changed the public perception of the Grimms' tales in Japan, where the tales had previously been circulating widely but mostly in heavily sanitized versions intended for a young audience.

Kiryū Misao is the pseudonym of two women, Tsutsumi Sachiko and Ueda Kayoko. Until Tsutsumi's death in 2003, they coauthored more than forty populist books about cruel and erotic episodes in European history and literature in which women, invariably characterized as femmes fatales, play the leading part. The preoccupation of their work with sex, crime, and other social taboos partakes of the subject matter of the so-called sensation novel of Victorian England; like the sensation novel, the main purpose of Grimm boom writings is to shock and entertain adult readers. It may be possible to draw a parallel between the historical backgrounds of these two societies; both the Grimm boom in the late 1990s in Japan and the publication phenomenon of the sensation novel in the 1860s and 1870s in Britain drew their energy from a popular reaction to the repressive moral climate of the time wherein the official emphasis on respectability and purity coexisted with the prevalence of moral corruption such as sexual exploitation and abuse. In the case of Japan, some of the contradictions seem to have their roots in the cultural conflict arising from the importation of Western ideas in which Japan has been engaged since the late nineteenth century. This conflict has been aggravated by the disjunction between the nationalistic values persisting since the wartime periods of the early twentieth century and the increasing social and cultural Americanization accompanying the rapid economic growth after the Second World War.

Kiryū's 1998 story collection consists of retellings of "Snow White," "Cinderella," "The Frog King," "Bluebeard," "Sleeping Beauty," and "The Juniper Tree." Each tale is followed by a synopsis of the psychoanalytic, folkloristic, sociohistorical, and literary interpretations of fairy tales offered by such Western scholars as Bettelheim, Tatar, Robert Darnton, and Carl-Heinz Mallet. "In the light of these scholars' varied interpretations," writes Kiryū in the preface, "we tried to re-create a more vivid and graphic version of Grimms' tales in our own fashion by keeping the cruel and violent expressions found in their first edition and by bringing out the depths of the psyche and the hidden meanings" (3). Although not properly acknowledged in the preface, however, Matsumoto's *Fairy Tales of Sinful Princesses* seems to have been a more direct source.[17]

What distinguishes the Grimm boom approach from a similar intertextual return to the older versions in the West represented by Carter's *The Bloody Chamber* is not only the former's exclusive emphasis on sensational subjects but also its Occidentalist reimagining of European fairy tales, as is exemplified in the illustrations for Kiryū's collection (figure 1.6). These illustrations follow the visual conventions of Japanese *shōjo* (girl) manga tradition established mainly by Ikeda Riyoko's *Berusaiyu no bara* (1972–73; *The Rose of Versailles*; sometimes abbreviated to *Berubara*), inspired by Stefan Zweig's biography of Marie Antoinette. Ikeda's manga depicts doll-like young women with large twinkling eyes adorned with long eyelashes, wavy long hair, slim elongated limbs, and a tiny waist, wearing long flowing dresses with masses of frills and ribbons and standing against a courtly background decorated with flowers—especially the roses of the title—and shiny ornaments. The *Berubara* aesthetics of the illustrations accompanying Kiryū's stories reflects one aspect of the Occidentalist fantasies circulating in Japan, fantasies that are a prominent feature of the Grimm boom in general. The obsession of the Grimm boom writings with violence and sexual transgression can be regarded as a projection of disavowed desires onto the cultural Other, which reflects the other side of Japan's longing admiration for the imagined West.

DREADFUL IN TRUTH

本当は恐ろしい
グリム童話

Kiryu Misao

桐生 操

FIGURE 1.6. Cover of *Hontō wa osoroshii Gurimu dōwa* (Grimms' Tales Are Really Horrific), by Kiryū Misao. Illustration by Yumimoto Sumika. Tokyo: KK Bestsellers, 1998. Courtesy of KK Bestsellers.

Kiryū's "Bluebeard: Another Key to the Forbidden Chamber" builds on Mallet's interpretation in *Kopf ab! Gewalt im Märchen* (1985) that Bluebeard's key is the key of the chastity belt metaphorically put on the wife's body. Kiryū also draws on Bettelheim's interpretation of the key as a phallic symbol and the blood on the key as the sign of defloration. Kiryū's emphasis, however, is on Bluebeard's wife's insatiable desire for sex and cruelty, which can be let loose by a duplicate key to the actual chastity belt that she is forced to wear by her jealous and misogynistic husband; the female body itself, therefore, is the forbidden chamber in this story. After having her husband murdered by her young lover, she becomes a female Bluebeard herself and takes to murdering innocent young men in bed, including the man who rescued her from Bluebeard. The heroine of Kiryū's "Bluebeard" recalls the Marquis de Sade's Juliette, a quintessential female sadist, whose cruelty surpasses even that of the cruelest of men, rather than the heroine in Carter's "The Bloody Chamber," who finds happiness in her reciprocal relationship with a gentle blind piano tuner. In whatever role they are cast, Kiryū's heroines are no passive victims of patriarchal society; their cunning and cruelty far exceed those of men, and they avidly follow their own Sadeian desires through to their "horrific" ends. As Carter argues in *The Sadeian Woman: An Exercise in Cultural History* (1979), however, women's pursuit of Sadeian desires, rather than liberating them from male dominance, ultimately serves the masculine paradigm of predator-victim dichotomy. *The Bloody Chamber,* published in the same year as *The Sadeian Woman,* can be seen as offering an alternative to the Sadeian logic of power, gender, and sexuality; as Margaret Atwood points out, "*The Bloody Chamber* may be read as a 'writing against' de Sade, a talking-back to him; and, above all, as an exploration of the possibilities for the kind of synthesis de Sade himself could never find because he wasn't even looking for it" (120). The Grimm boom writings also make use of this Sadeian pornographic approach to the fairy tale but, unlike Carter, they do so in a way that does not question the fundamental binary logic subjugating one gender—gender in the Sadeian sense is defined by power relations rather than anatomical difference—to another. Most of the Grimm boom works, although many of them were both produced and consumed by women, subscribe to this Sadeian-Shibusawan paradigm in which women are stereotyped either as an obedient, ever-victimized Justine or a predatory, supermasculine Juliette.

TAPPING INTO DIFFERENT DEPTHS

Since the 1990s, women writers have also begun to explore different narrative possibilities of the fairy tale. It is notable that contemporary Japanese female writers and artists rarely describe their works in terms of feminism even though the experience and expression specific to women have often been one of the chief concerns of their works. This shows the negative connotation of the word *feminism* in today's Japan, generally understood as women's—often characterized as hysterical—claim for equal rights, an issue central in second-wave feminism, which became active in the late 1960s. As a result of the strong backlash against feminism during the 1980s and the 1990s, the general understanding of feminism came to be restricted to this narrow stereotype propagated by the still predominantly male-oriented mass media.[18]

This does not mean that feminist scholarship has not developed in Japan since the 1970s, but it can be said that it has been considerably marginalized both in academia and in society compared to Western cultures. A new wave of feminist criticism that reconsiders the essentialist assumptions of second-wave feminism and incorporates theories of poststructuralism, deconstruction, postmodernism, and postcolonialism has also emerged. Nevertheless, critics tend to avoid using the term *feminism* in the titles and descriptions of their works, preferring to indicate their female-centered perspective by choosing titles and cover designs that imply female-oriented subjects and aesthetics.

One area of feminist criticism that has been developed in the field of Japanese cultural studies is an analysis of the representation of the shōjo. The field generally known as "girl studies" has recently emerged as a poststructuralist critique of the phallocentirc and heteronormative assumptions operating in modern and contemporary Japan. *Girl Reading Girl in Japan* (2010), a collection of essays in English by international scholars edited by Tomoko Aoyama and Barbara Hartley, gives an overview of the practices of reading and writing about girls in Japan since the 1980s. It is interesting that Honda Masuko's pioneering essay in 1980, translated in this collection as "The Genealogy of *Hirahira:* Liminality and the Girl," associates the subversive liminality of the girl figure with Sleeping Beauty and Snow White, the two fairy-tale heroines usually regarded as the epitome of female passivity by feminist scholars. Honda refers to the romanticized notion of girlhood as "the sleep of pupa awaiting transformation into a butterfly, a time spent in a closed world," which figures in fairy tales as "the hundred-year slumber of the Sleeping Beauty or the temporary death of Snow White," and claims that the girl's apparently passive state has the "double structure" of withdrawal and provocation: "The girl may try to avoid contact with the outside world when in her self-contained, inwardly converging state; nevertheless, her constant swaying and fluttering provokes and attracts the gaze of others" (Honda 20). The *hirahira* in the title is an onomatopoeia describing the fluttering motion of ribbons and frills, which are privileged aesthetic objects among girls usually considered frivolous and meaningless by men and those women who have grown out of such "girlish" tastes. If we follow Honda's argument, traditional fairy tales can be recuperated for girls' own reassertion of the hirahira aesthetic as valuable in its own right. This strategy can be found in the uses of fairy tales by some of the women writers discussed in Aoyama and Hartley's volume, such as Yoshimoto Banana (1964–), whose novels have been considered representative of such girl-centered aesthetics both in Japan and abroad.

Attractive and effective as such tactics are, however, they entail the danger of perpetuating the marginalization of women and the fairy tale, both of which are often connected with childishness in Japan. Moreover, the subversiveness of the hirahira aesthetic may—at least in some cases—be subsumed under the more commercialized and domesticated notion of *kawaii*, which has increasingly dominated Japanese culture since the 1970s and which has also spread globally as representative of contemporary Japanese culture. The sociologist Sharon Kinsella defines the term as follows: "Kawaii or 'cute' essentially means childlike; it celebrates sweet, adorable, innocent, pure, simple, genuine, gentle, vulnerable, weak, and inexperienced social behaviour and physical appearances" (220). Feminist recourse to hirahira, a notion perhaps too close to kawaii, could in some cases serve to reinforce the Western infantilization and feminization of Japanese culture. In my attempt to move beyond the male-oriented framework of both the Jungian-Kawaian and the Sadeian-Shibusawan interpretations of fairy tales, therefore, I will explore an approach to the fairy tale that resists the seductions of the hirahira tactics. The works of the four authors and artists I will discuss below represent Japanese women's uses of the fairy tale in a way that does not rely on the privileging of the figure of the shōjo, iconic of contemporary Japanese culture in a global context.

2

TAWADA YŌKO'S STORIES
of (UN)METAMORPHOSIS

The fairy tale has played a pivotal role in Tawada Yōko's writing from the earliest stages. Especially notable is her reworking of the animal bride and bridegroom tale, a tale type that has long existed in many cultures, Western and non-Western alike, with local variations. Tawada's fairy-tale adaptations self-consciously engage with the culture-specific narrative conventions found in the Asian variants of this tale as well as with its modern canonical form. In this chapter, I will first consider her uses of the motif of human-animal marriage in her oeuvre in connection with her cultural and linguistic doubleness. I will then closely examine how her novella, titled "Inumukoiri" (1993; translated into English as "The Bridegroom Was a Dog" in 1998), departs from the traditional tale by resisting and reorienting the desire for the dissolution of difference usually fulfilled at the end of the fairy tale.

WRITING BETWEEN TWO CULTURES AND TWO LANGUAGES

Tawada was born in a western suburb of Tokyo in 1960. After finishing her first degree in Russian literature at Waseda University in 1982, she moved to Hamburg and initially worked for a book distributor while learning German. While writing prose and poetry in both Japanese and German, she studied modern German literature at the University of Hamburg and received her doctorate from the University of Zurich with her thesis on the representations of toys, dolls, magic, and masks in the works of such writers as E. T. A. Hoffman, Franz Kafka, Walter Benjamin, and Michel Leiris. Although based in Germany, where she has lived for more than three decades, she has constantly been on the move, taking up writer-in-residence positions and giving readings and lectures in Japanese and German (and sometimes English) in various parts of the world. She now lives in Berlin.

From the beginning of her career, Tawada has always worked with two languages. Her first publication was a bilingual poetry collection—the original Japanese appearing alongside its German translation by Peter Pörtner—published in Germany in 1987 under the title *Nur da wo du bist da ist nichts* (Only There Where You Are Is Nothing). Two years later, her novella *Das Bad* (1989; The Bath), also translated from the Japanese, was published. Then in 1991, her first publication in Japanese, a novella titled "Kakato o nakushite" (translated into English as "Missing Heels" in 1998), was awarded the Gunzo Prize for New Writers. Her novella "The Bridegroom Was a Dog" won the Akutagawa Prize, Japan's top literary prize, in 1993. Her works written in German also began to be published: a novella, "Ein Gast" (1989; A Guest), a collection of prose and poetry, *Wo Europa anfängt* (1991; *Where Europe Begins*), and a play, *Die Kranichmaske, die bei Nacht strahlt* (1993; The Mask of the Crane, Which Shines at Night; Japanese title *Yoru hikaru tsuru no kamen*), which was first performed in German-speaking regions and then traveled to Japan in her own translation. In 1996, she was awarded the Adelbert von Chamisso Prize, a literary award for authors writing in German whose mother tongue and cultural background are non-German. Since then, she has been awarded several major prizes both in Japan and in Germany, including the Tanizaki Prize and the Goethe Medal. Her work now spans a wide range of media, including collaboration with artists, photographers, musicians, and theater and dance companies.

Her first book in English translation was published by Kodansha International in 1998 as *The Bridegroom Was a Dog*. It is a collection of three novellas, "The Bridegroom Was a Dog," "Missing Heels," and "The Gotthard Railway" (1996; original title, "Gottoharuto tetsudō"), all translated from the Japanese by Margaret Mitsutani. In 2002, the New York-based publisher New Directions began to publish Tawada's work, beginning with *Where Europe Begins*, which contains ten stories, two translated from the Japanese and eight from the German, and which has a preface by the Germany-born film director Wim Wenders. *Facing the Bridge* (2007) consists of three novellas translated from the Japanese, including "Saint George and the Translator" (1993; original title "Arufabetto no kizuguchi," literally, "the wound in the alphabet"). *The Naked Eye* (2009; original title, *Tabi o suru hadaka no me*) was her first novel-length work to appear in English. In 2012, *The Bridegroom Was a Dog* was reissued as part of the New Directions Pearls, a series of short works of contemporary world literature.

It is telling that, even after entering the contemporary canon of world literature,[1] her work still tends to be Orientalized in English-speaking cultures, as is evident from the blurb on the back cover of the New Directions edition of *The Bridegroom Was a Dog*: "an odd romance ensues— simmering with secrets, chivalry, and sex." As this chapter will make clear, distorting the emphasis in this way can deflect the reader from engaging with Tawada's radical subversion of the conventions of both Western and Japanese fairy tales.

Tawada's interest in the fairy tale is multifaceted. "Where Europe Begins" (1991), the title story of her second book in English, is an account of a young Japanese woman's journey to Moscow on the Trans-Siberian Railway. The text consists of a mosaic of various kinds of narratives, such as the heroine's reminiscences about her childhood, her parents' life stories, the stories told to her by her grandmother and her mother, Siberian fairy tales she reads on the train, excerpts from her diary, travelogue, and letters, and the account of her journey she gives to a woman whose relationship with her is unexplained. These narrative fragments, all of which are stories about women told by and to women across different generations, cultures, and languages, are intertwined with each other in a subtle—and some-times disturbing—way to weave a complex tapestry of women's lives, a part of history that has often been made invisible in official discourses. For example, the story told by her grandmother about the connection between the traditional Japanese doll called *kokeshi,* which literally means "make-the-child-go-away" (*Where Europe Begins* 142), and the old practice of infanticide among poor peasants in Japan casts an ominous shadow over an apparently peaceful scene on the train in which a Russian boy is playing with a Matryoshka doll. The narrator notes that this Russian doll, which has the figure of a smaller doll, a family member, nested inside that of a bigger one, is said to have been modeled after a kokeshi, the doll made as a memorial to a murdered child. The story of the kokeshi also resonates with the Samoyedic fairy tale that the narrator reads on the train and quotes in full: in this tale, the mother sacrifices her child to appease the anger of the Empress of Fire. Arising from these fragments are women's conflicted feelings toward their children, which have largely been suppressed in the normative discourse on motherhood. Tawada states elsewhere that she used Siberian fairy tales in "Where Europe Begins" because she wanted to give voice to the Siberian people, whose history, like that of women's, has been neglected in official history and has survived mainly in the oral tradition ("A Conversation"). Siberia assumes a special significance for Tawada as a vast territory lying between the East and the West, an evocative space that she crossed by train when she first went to Europe.

Her novella "Missing Heels," in which a young Japanese woman becomes an "official mail-order bride" to a stranger living in an unspecified European country (*The Bridegroom Was a Dog* 75), can be read as a variation on the Bluebeard story. The moment she first arrives at "Central Station" in the new country, she loses her balance and falls over on her suitcase, which somehow results in her losing her heels—not those of her shoes but of her own feet. She feels relieved when she finds out that the three hard-boiled eggs she has been carrying in her suitcase are still intact. Although she starts living with her husband in his large house, the heroine, as in "Cupid and Psyche," is never allowed to see him; all she can see is his two eyeballs staring at her from the dark corridor. Despite this unwelcoming situation, she decides to learn about the everyday customs of her husband's country by registering for the "General Training School for Beginners" (81). At the end of the story, she breaks into his locked room with the help of a locksmith in order to confront her husband and to retrieve her hard-boiled eggs and notebooks, which have gone missing, only to discover a squid, which she recognizes as her husband, lying dead on the floor. The hard-boiled eggs she carries evoke the motif of the broken egg as a telltale sign of the wife's disobedience in the Grimms' "Fitcher's Bird," a variant of "Bluebeard." The number of eggs also coincides with the number of sisters in the Grimms' story. It is as if Tawada's heroine were hard-boiled enough not to be afraid of betraying her transgression to her husband.

On the other hand, the motif of missing heels—a faint echo of the bleeding heels of Cinderella's wicked stepsister—can be interpreted as a metaphor for the linguistic, cultural, and social displacement the heroine experiences when she steps alone into a totally unfamiliar environment. In

"Missing Heels," the otherness of the mysterious bridegroom in such traditional stories as "Beauty and the Beast" and "Bluebeard" is pushed to its absurd extreme—a squid does not bear any symbolic significance in Japanese folklore and mythology—so as to foreground the disorienting and destabilizing sense of one's own otherness that one feels upon being thrown into a foreign environment, as the author herself may have felt when she moved to Germany at the age of twenty-two. Tawada's work uses the fairy-tale narrative in order to defamiliarize the language and the narratives that make up the reader's ordinary perception of the self and the world. As the Canadian American writer Rivka Galchen points out, Tawada's defamiliarization of the fairy tale is intimately linked with the experience of living in a foreign-language environment: "Often in Tawada's work, one has the feeling of having wandered into a mythology that is not one's own. This is, of course, precisely what it feels like to speak in a non-mother tongue."

Her play *The Mask of the Crane, Which Shines at Night* also uses the motif of the human-animal marriage as a metaphor for the difficulty of living with the cultural Other. One of the main characters is a man called Brother who was once married to a turtle and is now married to a shellfish, which connects this story with two nonhuman bride tales in Japanese folklore, "Urashima Tarō" and "Hamaguri nyōbō" (The Clam Wife). In a widespread version of "Urashima Tarō," a fisherman rescues a turtle and is rewarded with a visit to an undersea palace, where he is welcomed by the beautiful princess, who turns out to be the turtle he saved. Like the heroine in "Beauty and the Beast," the fisherman starts missing his homeland and, while temporarily back at home, he breaks his promise not to open the box given by the princess and is never allowed to return to the palace, losing her for good. Less widely known is "The Clam Wife," the story of a man who receives an unexpected visit from a beautiful woman and marries her. Although he is told never to peep in while she is cooking, he becomes terribly curious as to why her miso soup tastes so good. One day, he spies on her and sees her urinating into a cooking pot. The infuriated husband tells her to go away, upon which she transforms herself into a clam and disappears into the sea.

In Tawada's play, Brother's two wives apparently retain their nonhuman form during their marriage. In his first marriage, Brother agonizes not over his wife's nonhuman form but over his own inability to lay eggs like turtles. His agony foregrounds the fundamental species-specific and sexual differences between himself and his wife in a way that, unlike many animal bride stories, does not automatically give privilege to his status as a human male. In his second marriage, he breaks his promise not to look in the kitchen while his wife is cooking and finds her urinating into a pot of soup. Unlike the clam wife in the folktale, however, his wife does not notice him watching her, and he continues to enjoy her exquisite soup. In a play within a play, Brother also takes on the role of the mask-wearing crane of the title, evoking "Tsuru nyōbō" (The Crane Wife), a tale about a man who marries a crane disguised as a beautiful woman. In *The Mask of the Crane, Which Shines at Night,* the folkloric motif of the nonhuman partner again works as a metaphor for the disorienting otherness engendered by cultural and sexual difference.

In her story collection *Futakuchi otoko* (1998; The Man with Two Mouths; originally published as *Nīdāzakusen monogatari* in 1997–98),[2] Tawada turns to German folklore. In the title story, a group of Japanese tourists on a guided tour through Lower Saxony meet the legendary medieval trickster Till Eulenspiegel in real life. In this story, Till figures as an outsider both culturally and linguistically; throughout the tour, no one except the bilingual Japanese tour guide can understand his words because he speaks only in German (although the reader can understand his words since the text itself is all written in Japanese). The "two mouths" in the title, therefore, partly stand for the two languages coexisting in the story.[3] In Tawada's own theatrical adaptation of this story, the actors speak either in Japanese or in German, according to their roles, without subtitles. In her readings and performances, Tawada sometimes employs this bilingual style, juxtaposing Japanese and German without translation, making the sounds of two different languages clash and resonate with each other so that the members of the audience are encouraged to make their own interpretation of the sounds, whose meanings they may or may not understand. Tawada thus foregrounds not only cultural but also linguistic otherness in her reworking of folkloric material. Such experiments with spoken language also show Tawada's concern with today's oral storytelling culture, which has increasingly become more multilingual and multicultural as the world becomes more globally mobile.

"Fuefuki otoko" (The Piper),[4] another story in the same collection, refracts the Grimms' "The Children of Hamelin" by fragmenting the narrative from the perspectives of various characters both in and outside the story, including the piper, the children, their mothers, and the Brothers Grimm themselves, whose account of the historical incident in Hamelin in 1284, which resulted in the disappearance of 130 children, is quoted in full. Tawada's multivoiced retelling of "The Children of Hamelin" ends by assigning the authorial role to the least likely character in the story; the closing fragment reveals that the whole story was produced by a rat swimming around inside the word processor.

Tawada's "Saint George and the Translator" recasts the legend of the dragon slayer in the West, which can be traced back to the ancient Greek myth of Perseus and Andromeda and whose fairy-tale equivalent, the "Dragon Slayer" tale type (ATU 300), is regarded as "the archetype of the fairy tale" by Vladimir Propp in his *Morphology of the Folktale* (1928) (89). The narrator-protagonist of "Saint George and the Translator" is a young Japanese woman who goes to a small island to translate "Der wunde Punkt im Alphabet" (1989),[5] Anne Duden's rewriting of the legend of Saint George and the dragon. By following Walter Benjamin's claim in "The Task of the Translator" that a "real translation . . . may be achieved, above all, by a literal rendering of the syntax which proves words rather than sentences to be the primary element of the translator" (79) and taking it one step further, the heroine translates Duden's text into Japanese word by word, literally punctuating after each word with the Japanese equivalent of a comma and never using a period to mark the end of a sentence. This excessively literal translation produces a radically fragmented and monstrously serpentine text, a style that, as Tawada's English translator Margaret Mitsutani points out ("Translator's Afterword" 183–84), can be interpreted as a metaphor for the body of the dragon, an imaginary creature composed of fragments from various animals, an age-old symbol in many cultures of people's fears and desires. As the heroine's translation progresses, her body begins to transform gradually—her right nipple, for example, suddenly cracks into four parts—and, when she finally finishes translating the whole story, she finds herself turned into a dragon. The story ends as the translator-dragon runs desperately toward the sea in order to escape the men on the island who are now transformed into multiple Saint Georges brandishing swords.

In Tawada's rewriting of the dragon-slayer tale, the heroine identifies herself not with the princess to be rescued—her friend George, who she believes may follow her to the island, never actually turns up—but with the imaginary beast to be slain by the hero, which connects her with such mythical female monsters as Medusa and the Sphinx who, as Teresa de Lauretis states in *Alice Doesn't: Feminism, Semiotics, Cinema* (1984), "have survived inscribed in hero narratives, in someone else's story, not their own." De Lauretis argues that traditional stories of women, myths of females monsters, and fairy tales such as "Snow White" and "Cinderella" are not their own stories but are embedded in masculine desire: "they are figures or markers of positions—places and topoi—through which the hero and his story move to their destination and to accomplish meaning" (109). Tawada's heroine, however, may follow a different path because here her act of translation is bestowed with the power to transform the existing system of language by marrying two different languages; in other words, she uses her ability to move between two languages to create a new interlingual language that will enable her to tell a new story.

Thus, Tawada's work recasts the fairy tale in order to articulate the radical otherness that destabilizes established notions of language, culture, and identity. In what follows, I will analyze how her "The Bridegroom Was a Dog" reworks the animal bridegroom tale type in such a way that it displaces the canonized versions of this tale type both in Japan and in the West.

NATURALIZING FEMALE SELF-SACRIFICE: "THE CRANE WIFE"

The heroine of "The Bridegroom Was a Dog" says to her pupils at her cram school: "Maybe the only story you know about a human being marrying an animal is 'The Crane Wife,' but there's another one called 'The Bridegroom Was a Dog'" (13). She then goes through a catalogue of variants of this now rather obscure folktale, whose title is also the title of the story she is in. In order to provide a context for Tawada's radical reworking of this tale type, I will begin by giving an overview of animal bride and bridegroom tales in Japanese folklore in comparison with their Western counterparts, focusing especially on the representation of nature and femininity in "The Crane Wife," the best-known variant of this tale type in Japan.

Traditional Japanese animal bride and bridegroom tales generally end with the separation of the couple when the animal partner leaves the human protagonist for good. This pattern offers a striking contrast to the tale type's European counterparts, which tend to end with a happy marriage after the animal bride or bridegroom is transformed back into her or his original human form. Ozawa Toshio summarizes Japanese animal bride and bridegroom tales as follows: "In Japanese animal bride and bridegroom tales, animals visit the human world from the undefined world of nature and establish some kind of relationship with human beings. There are three patterns of development, in which the animals eventually (1) leave on their own accord, (2) are expelled by the human beings and return to the undefined world of nature, or (3) are killed by the human beings" (*Mukashibanashi no kosumoroji* 235). In all three cases, states Ozawa, the story ends by reestablishing the clear boundary between the human and the nonhuman that had been broken down by marriage at the beginning of the story. As in European tales, the order of the human world is recovered in the end, but this ending usually entails a sense of loss and evanescence.[6]

Paradoxically, another characteristic of Japanese tales of human-animal marriage is the assumed continuity between the human and the nonhuman, which apparently contradicts the final dissolution of the human-animal union. Unlike in many European fairy tales, transformations into and from animals are rarely explained in terms of magic and seem to be taken for granted as a natural course of events. In "Kitsune nyōbō" (The Fox Wife), for example, the woman assumes her fox form before her husband's eyes merely by turning around. In some tales, transformation simply does not occur, and human beings marry their nonhuman partners, who remain in their original form throughout the story until their eventual death or disappearance.

Ozawa attributes this closeness between humans and animals in Japanese tales to the traditional animistic view that every organism in nature has its own meaning and power and that human beings are also part of nature (*Mukashibanashi no kosumoroji* 194). At the same time, the final ejection of animal partners in these tales also shows the strong awareness of the demarcation between the human world and nature (245). Ozawa suggests that Japanese animal bride and bridegroom tales reflect a worldview located between animistic cultures; he cites as an example Inuit tales in which human beings accept their nonhuman partners in their original form—such as a large crab—and live happily ever after, comparing this to the anthropocentric Christian culture, in which humans are clearly distinguished from animals.[7] In Japanese tales, animal partners remain animals until the end of the story but, unlike the crab husband in the Inuit tale, they inevitably leave the human world after revealing their original animal identity. Some European stories that have maintained strong pre-Christian roots, such as the legend of Melusine, exhibit a similar structure to Japanese tales. Melusine, a water spirit, marries her husband in the guise of a human girl and asks him not to spy on her in the bath. She disappears the moment he peeks in and discovers her original form as a serpent from the waist down. Many nonhuman partners in European fairy tales, on the other hand, turn out to be human beings turned into animals by a curse; their otherness, in other words, is only superficial and temporary.

Interestingly, Ozawa also observes that Japanese tales about animal brides mostly follow either pattern (1) or (2), whereas animal bridegroom tales almost always follow pattern (3). He deduces that female animals are generally considered to be harmless once they return to the world of nature, whereas male animals are seen as a threat even after their ejection from the human world and must be killed (*Mukashibanashi no kosumoroji* 242–43). I argue, however, that it is also possible to interpret this gender-specific pattern as a reflection of the culturally dominant view that relegates femininity to nature, an "undefined" sphere to be kept at bay in order to maintain the order of human—that is, masculine—society. As I will argue below, this interpretation explains one reason why "The Crane Wife," in which a male protagonist marries a female animal, became canonized during the period of Japan's postwar rapid economic growth, largely driven by a masculine desire for progress and self-aggrandization.

Among various animal bride and bridegroom tales in Japan, "The Crane Wife" has become the most popular, especially since the playwright Kinoshita Junji (1914–2006) adapted it for the stage mainly for an adult audience in 1949, giving it the tile *Yūzuru* (*Twilight Crane*; English translation in 1956). "The Crane Wife" is now one of the most widely known folktales in Japan and has been frequently adapted for other media including film, opera, contemporary dance, and commercial advertisements, not to mention children's books and animations. Kinoshita's play is based on the version recorded in Niigata, a northern region of Japan, and published in 1942 in a tale collection edited by Yanagita Kunio (1875–1962), the founder of Japanese folkloristics. In this canonical version, a poor man rescues an injured crane and releases it. A couple of days later, a beautiful woman appears at his doorstep and asks him to marry her. He does so, and she offers to weave a cloth if he promises never to watch her making it. He takes the fine brocade woven by her to the emperor, who pays a huge sum for it. The husband begs her to make another cloth and, while she is weaving, he peeks in and finds a crane plucking her own feathers and weaving them into the loom. Seeing his betrayal, the crane flies away, never to return (64–65).

"The Crane Wife" contains the tale type of "Grateful Animals" (ATU 554), in which animals repay the kindness offered by human beings. In some variants, an elderly couple rather than a single man help the crane and adopt her as their daughter, which is the form often considered more appropriate for the child readership today because of its unmistakably non-sexual quality; it removes the element of romance, which is rarely present in Japanese folktales except for animal bride and bridegroom tales, and emphasizes the theme of requited kindness instead. In all variants of "The Crane Wife," however, kindness is rewarded only temporarily—until the protagonist discovers the true identity of the visitor. The magic spell is broken at the end of the story but, unlike in "Beauty and the Beast," the husband in "The Crane Wife" ends up losing his beloved wife, who turns back into her original animal form and returns to her realm for good.

The tragic separation of the couple is caused by the husband's violation of the taboo against viewing. This "Forbidden Chamber" motif, classified as C611 in Stith Thompson's *Motif-Index of Folk-Literature*, can be found also in "Bluebeard" tales, but "The Crane Wife" resembles the story of Melusine more closely in its representation of the nonhuman female as the absolute Other. The important difference, however, is that "The Crane Wife" stresses themes of female gratitude and self-sacrifice absent from the Melusine legend; this emphasis works to obscure the dominating and destructive nature of the human husband's violation of the taboo against viewing her private self.

In their analysis of Japanese folkloric representations of nonhuman brides, Jason Davis and Mio Bryce point out that Japanese animal bride stories are often about the victimized female Other: "A non-human bride's permanent marriage to a human is only possible through the total suppression of her non-human identity, in other words, the necessity for her total social conformity; the total domestication of her as a resource. This means that there is no place for her to authentically live as she truly is. Despite the animistic closeness between humans and non-humans, which is often seen as a characteristic of Japanese culture, the stories expose an inability to recognise and deal with Otherness (e.g., Nature/female) as a respectable partner" (204).

Kinoshita's play makes this contrast between male desire and female self-sacrifice more explicit. The protagonist of *Twilight Crane* is portrayed as a man who becomes so obsessed with money that he does not even notice his wife's increasingly failing health as he demands her to weave more and more cloth. The play is intended and generally interpreted as a criticism of postwar Japanese society, driven by greed and materialism that exploit and disregard the power of love and nature. This view, which came to affect the general understanding of the original folktale, however, tells only the male side of the story. "The Crane Wife," as Davis and Bryce claim, can be read as a patriarchal society's nostalgia for nature, represented here as a female animal, from which the "civilized" human world receives benefits but from which it remains ultimately separate. By conflating nature with femininity, the story works to naturalize female self-sacrifice as a necessary component of the development of civilization at the cost of nature.

As I will discuss below, however, there have always been other variants of the animal bride and bridegroom tale type in Japan. Tawada's retelling brings into play those forgotten versions, which invite a radically different interpretation of nature, femininity, and otherness from the one endorsed by the canonized tale.

HOW THE DOG CAME TO LICK THE PRINCESS'S BOTTOM

Unlike "The Crane Wife," the story of the dog bridegroom was neglected by the early folklorists and did not enter the modern canon of folktales in Japan.[8] A typical Japanese dog bridegroom tale begins with the mother promising the dog that he can marry her daughter, a child as the tale begins, if he licks the girl's bottom clean after she defecates. When the daughter grows up, the dog demands to marry her, and the two go away to live in the mountains. One day, a passing huntsman kills the dog in secret and then marries the widow. After the couple has seven children, the huntsman confesses the murder to his wife, upon which she kills him out of revenge.

In her essay on her own "The Bridegroom Was a Dog," Tawada states that it was inspired by a folkloristic analysis of this often neglected variant of the animal bridegroom tale found throughout Asia. While expressing her intense dislike for the kind of "wholesomeness" and "cleanliness" glowing on the face of the conquering hero of "Momotarō" (*Katakoto no uwagoto* 18), a canonical tale widely used for war propaganda, as I pointed out in chapter 1, Tawada claims that she found the dog bridegroom tale interesting because of the motif of the close physical contact between the princess and the dog, which recurs in other variants throughout Asia. In other words, she was attracted by this folktale because it shows how the same motifs, peculiar as they seem, can be found widely among diverse cultures in Asia. This Asia-focused comparative perspective seems to stem from her own experience of being categorized as an Asian, rather than as a Japanese, by people living outside Japan, a recurrent subject throughout her oeuvre. Her reworking of the dog bridegroom tale informed by a comparative folkloristic perspective can be seen as a critique of the nationalistic uses to which folktales have sometimes been put in Japan, as in other countries. Her aversion to "Momotarō," a tale once used to advocate Japan's military invasion of other parts of Asia, seems to stem from her postcolonial standpoint and her transnational solidarity with diverse yet closely interrelated narrative traditions in Asia.

The essay that inspired Tawada to rewrite the dog bridegroom tale is Fukuda Akira's comparative analysis of this tale type in Japan and other Asian countries, published in 1975. In this study, Fukuda classifies Asian variants into four types and compares them with the Japanese variant. He first relates this tale type to a clan origin myth found in the mountainous regions of southern China, Vietnam, Laos, and Thailand. In this variant, which is generally referred to as the *Pan Gu* legend after the name of the dog and which Fukuda calls type A, the emperor promises to give his daughter's hand in marriage to anyone who can kill a hostile leader and bring back his head. A dog returns with the leader's head and marries the emperor's daughter. In turn, their children marry each other and become the progenitors of a clan. In the variant type B, found among the Moken, sea nomads inhabiting the areas on and near the west coast of Thailand, and the Seediq, a Taiwanese aboriginal people, the woman and the dog marry and live on a desert island. After the dog's death, she tricks her son into marrying her without revealing her identity. Type C, a variant found in Indonesia and on Hainan Island in China, is similar to type B but includes the motif of patricide by the hybrid son of the woman and the dog. In type D, found in Okinawa, a region in southern Japan that was originally part of an independent kingdom called the Ryūkyū Kingdom until the late nineteenth century, a fisherman kills the dog, marries the woman, and has seven children with her. When she learns about the murder, she dies of sorrow among the dog's bones.

The most notable difference between the Japanese and Okinawan variants and the other Asian variants may be the absence of the motif of overt bestiality in the former. Fukuda assumes that types A, B, and C first reached Okinawa and then spread to and diffused throughout Japan. The Okinawan tale (type D) replaces the interspecies reproduction with the marriage between humans, as in all Japanese dog bridegroom tales, but it does not include the wife's murder of her human husband out of revenge, a motif characteristic of the Japanese variant. The Okinawan tale, therefore, can be regarded as a transitional form between types A, B, and C and the Japanese variant, in the latter of which the motif of bestiality seems to have left its curious trace in the episode of the dog licking the girl's bottom.

Another interesting difference is that the Japanese and Okinawan tales end with a moral absent in the other Asian variants: "Never trust your wife even after having seven children with her." Fukuda points out that this moral, originally derived from an old Chinese poem, was a popular saying in Japan, considered to be an incisive description of the fundamentally conflicting relation of the sexes. This misogynous moral was incorporated into the tale as a kind of folk wisdom and served to reinforce the tale's folk authenticity. As Fukuda's tautological dictum has it, "[T]he legitimacy of the folktale is proved by the 'saying' while the authenticity of the 'saying' is proved by the folktale" (64). However, in the Japanese case, the reason why this odd moral—which puts an unfair emphasis on the woman's revenge murder at the end over the man's initial murder—came to be attached to the dog bridegroom tale may be explained by the tale's older form as an origin myth that ends with the mother's seduction of her son by deception, a motif converted into the warning against the deceptive wife in the Japanese and Okinawan variants.

The most significant difference between these dog bridegroom tales in Asia and the typical European animal bridegroom tales is the absence of either transformation or revelation in the former. "Beauty and the Beast," classified as subtype C of "The Search for the Lost Husband" (ATU 425), ends with the nonhuman husband's transformation into a human. The most widely known version of "Beauty and the Beast" was written by Madame Jeanne-Marie Leprince de Beaumont and published in *Le magasin des enfants* in 1756. In de Beaumont's version, Beauty stays in the Beast's palace in order to save her father, whose life is threatened by the Beast when he plucks a rose from the Beast's garden for his youngest daughter. Beauty grows fond of the kind-hearted Beast, but she keeps refusing his nightly marriage proposal. While Beauty is visiting her sick father, her two evil sisters conspire to keep her longer in order to make her break her promise to the Beast. Upon returning, she finds the Beast on the verge of death out of despair. She begs him not to die and promises to marry him. The Beast turns into a beautiful prince, which is revealed to be his original form. They marry and live happily ever after. In the much older subtypes, "Cupid and Psyche" (ATU 425A) and "East of the Sun, West of the Moon" (ATU 425B), the heroine marries either an animal or an invisible bridegroom, who turns out to be a handsome youth at the end of the story.

There are also similarities, however; both Asian and European versions of the animal bridegroom tale end with the disappearance of the animal. The dog is ultimately replaced with a human in all the versions of the dog bridegroom tale in Asia, just as the nonhuman bridegroom in the "Beauty and the Beast" stories always turns into a human. In either case, the boundary between human and nonhuman is reestablished, with the protagonist remaining on the human side. The ending of the Japanese dog bridegroom tale, however, suggests the heroine's refusal to fit into this pattern; her murder of the huntsman reaffirms her union with the dog. The subversiveness of her desire is mitigated by the rather strained moral about female deception added to the ending.

The apparent happiness achieved by the Beast's recuperation of his human form at the end of "Beauty and the Beast" has been questioned by recent fairy-tale studies and rewritings in the West. Cristina Bacchilega, for example, claims that the Beast's transformation into a handsome prince "betrays [Beauty's] desire and decision-making" and calls it "a magic trick which leaves *almost* no trace of Beauty's desires and losses" (*Postmodern Fairy Tales* 81). In "The Tiger's Bride," Angela Carter's rewriting of "Beauty and the Beast" in *The Bloody Chamber and Other Stories*, it is not the animal bridegroom but his human bride who finally goes through a metamorphosis—into a tiger—an ending that subverts the anthropocentric and androcentric perspective underlying de Beaumont's tale.

Tawada states that the motifs she likes best among various Asian versions are the dog's licking of the heroine's bottom and her unhesitating murder of the huntsman in revenge for the killing of her dog husband, both of which only appear in the Japanese variant. The absence of any description of the heroine's dislike of the dog's licking indicates that she does not suffer any inner conflict over her peculiar physical contact with the dog. This lack of conflict over the nonhuman nature of the partner provides a striking contrast to both European animal bridegroom tales and canonized Japanese tales exemplified by "The Crane Wife," in which the nonhuman form of the partner is perceived as an insuperable obstacle to a happy ending.

At the same time, Tawada deplores the absence of the motif of mother-son incest in the Japanese tales, a motif that she incorporates into her rewriting with the gender of the child reversed, thereby subverting the heteronormativity of the tale. She states: "I put together only the elements that appealed to me and made up a version of my own" (*Katakoto no uwagoto* 19–20). By reviving and reorienting these buried elements, Tawada's version remaps this popular tale type.

Tawada's "The Bridegroom Was a Dog" is intended as a structural variation on the traditional dog bridegroom tale which, as we have seen, has maintained basically the same pattern however variable its details may be. This patchwork of the variants of the old tale type begins to form its own pattern when woven together with Tawada's creative imagination. She describes the gripping structuring power of the dog bridegroom tale as follows: "While I was writing a novel last year, this version vividly sprang into my mind, sneaked up from behind, took over the novel, and transformed it into 'The Bridegroom Was a Dog'" (*Katakoto no uwagoto* 20). This long-forgotten tale of human-animal marriage, as I will discuss below, also generates and shapes the narrative desires of the characters in Tawada's story.

IN THE MIDST OF METAMORPHOSIS: "THE BRIDEGROOM WAS A DOG"

Kitamura Mitsuko, the heroine of "The Bridegroom Was a Dog," tells her pupils different versions of the dog bridegroom tale spread throughout Asia. These stories are then disseminated throughout the town by the children, who go home and try to reproduce what they have heard from their cram school teacher. To their mothers' frustration, however, they can tell the stories only in a fragmentary form. The mothers then exchange the fragments with each other, and there emerge two versions of the tale, which they call the "forest version" and the "desert island version," roughly corresponding to the Japanese variant and the Asian variant type B respectively. To the children, the motif of incest contained in type B "seemed perfectly natural" (14), and it is the episode of the dog licking the princess's bottom clean that leaves the most vivid and sensuous impression on them, so that they start mimicking the licking dog when they eat ice cream, for example, which disgusts their mothers. To the mothers, on the other hand, the folk origin of the story gives Mitsuko's storytelling some kind of moral authority: "[S]omeone who was taking a class in folklore at the Culture Center swore she'd seen that story in one of her books, so it must be authentic, which was a comforting thought to the other mothers" (15–16). Although they seem disturbed by the episodes of the licking dog and the mother-son incest, the mothers feel reassured by the knowledge that it is just another version of the traditional, "authentic" story, like "The Crane Wife." It is interesting that, in Tawada's story, the oral transmission of stories from one generation to the next takes place in the reverse direction, that is, from children to mothers, which subverts the notion of storytelling as a form of moral education and instead foregrounds the nonhierarchical and more pleasurable aspect of oral storytelling.

Mitsuko also tells her pupils her eccentric opinion about the use of tissue paper, which they report to their mothers as follows: "Miss Kitamura says wiping your nose with snot paper you've already used once is nice, because it's so soft and warm and wet, but when you use it a third time to wipe yourself when you go to the bathroom, it feels even better" (11–12). This real-life episode about Mitsuko and the "snot paper" becomes mixed up with the story about the dog licking the girl's bottom and begins to haunt the minds not only of the children but also of their mothers: "[N]o matter how determined they were not to imagine their child's beautiful teacher sitting on the toilet wiping herself with that lovely moist tissue, Miss Kitamura's smiling face invariably rose before them" (12). As Katrin Amann points out, "Mitsuko's world is the world of physical sensation and perception," centered around excretion and sexuality, whereas "the mothers, as the collective appellation indicates, belong to the world devoid of the body" (112). As the bodily motifs of the folktale begin to take on lives of their own, the boundaries between the clean and the unclean, the human and the nonhuman, and reality and fantasy become blurred, disturbing the order of the seemingly respectable community.

"The Bridegroom Was a Dog" revolves around various binary oppositions. The story is set in a town in contemporary Japan, probably modeled on the western suburb of Tokyo where Tawada grew up. The town is made up of two distinct areas. The northern part consists of public housing complexes developed in the 1960s while the southern district is said to have prospered as a rice-growing area along the river since ancient times, until the development in the northern area began, and it still has the remains of "human dwellings that dated back farther than you could imagine" (19). It is in the south side of the town that Mitsuko arrives, seemingly from nowhere, on her mountain bike and opens a cram school for schoolchildren in an old house that she rents from a farmer. Her pupils come from the new housing complexes in the northern district, populated mostly by young couples who have seldom stepped into the southern area themselves. As her family name Kitamura (*kita* means "north," and *mura* means "village") indicates, Mitsuko is an intermediate figure between the modernized north and the archaic south.

Mitsuko crosses not only spatial but also epistemological boundaries. Upon finding out her age from their children, the mothers face a question of classification: "[W]hen a woman doesn't have any children, the age of thirty-nine—past youth yet not quite over the hill—makes it hard to know what category to put her in" (18). Mitsuko is perceived by the mothers as an in-between being, neither young nor old, educated but uncivilized, and beautiful but not feminine in any conventional way. In other words, she is seen as an otherworldly visitor who does not belong to their clean, clear-cut "reality" and therefore comes to function as a kind of safety valve for their repressed desires. Her first name also suggests her role as a mysterious outsider; although Mitsuko is written in *hiragana,* one possible rendering of *mitsu* in a Chinese character is 密, which means "secrecy" and "intimacy." Tawada's story plays with gothic narrative conventions as what follows in the story can be read as a fantasy arising from the unconscious of those housewives living their obsessively hygienic and decorous lives in the standardized housing complex. It also shows the process by which a long-forgotten version of the animal bridegroom tale stirs up their deeply buried desires, instigating them to weave stories around those whom they consider different or not quite as "human" as themselves.

Mitsuko's physical beauty raises people's expectations for an old familiar plot. The head teacher of the elementary school expresses his bewilderment: "It's unusual for a beautiful woman to look that happy. I thought traditional beauties were supposed to be sad and lonely" (12). Despite her appearance, however, Mitsuko resists being classified as a traditional beauty such as those who appear in popular Japanese tales like "The Crane Wife" and "Yuki onna" (Snow Woman), the latter being another tale of marriage between different kinds in which the beautiful snow spirit melts away when her human partner breaks his promise not to tell anyone about her.[9] In Kawai Hayao's view, the male protagonist's eventual loss of his beloved wife in "The Crane Wife" is not perceived as a punishment for him as the story achieves an aesthetically satisfying effect of *aware,* or a sense of beauty with sorrow, through the realization of the pathos of nature, which is valued above the realization of a harmonious marital union: "It is a Japanese cultural paradigm that a woman must disappear in order for sorrow to complete the sense of beauty" (*The Japanese Psyche* 22). Importantly, this sense of sorrowful beauty is achieved at the cost of the animal wife, who represents such feminine virtues as self-sacrifice, obedience, diligence, and beauty, virtues also valued in the heroine of de Beaumont's "Beauty and the Beast."[10] Therefore, the *aware* paradigm and the happily-ever-after paradigm, although they appear to be opposites, have the same effect in terms of the suppression of female subjectivity. The heroine of Tawada's story, however, pays no attention to any of the gender stereotypes endorsed in these canonized stories and continues her happy, unconventional, and independent life on the south side of the town, disseminating stories through the medium of the children traversing the two areas "through the gap in the fence around Mitsuko's house" ("The Bridegroom Was a Dog" 20).

The story takes a magical turn when an immaculately groomed and muscular man in his late twenties arrives at Mitsuko's house out of the blue and invites himself in, saying, "I'm here to stay." He then introduces himself: "You can call me Taro. Under the circumstances, it mightn't be advisable to use my real name, but I can't think of any other" (25). Since Tarō, like Tom or Jack in English tales, is a generic name for male characters in traditional Japanese tales such as "Momotarō" and "Urashima Tarō," this revelation of his "real name" self-reflexively confirms his fairy-tale status.[11] Moreover, his affinity with the dog in the folktale is also indicated by the first of the two Chinese characters for Tarō, 太, which is very similar in form to the character for the dog, 犬, as well as by his family name, Iinuma, which includes the sound *inu,* the Japanese word for dog.

After this abrupt self-introduction, Tarō immediately sets about performing one of his husbandly duties:

> [T]he man slipped off her shorts as easily as drawing a handkerchief out of his sleeve, laid her on her back, and very politely, still in his shirt and pants, fitted his body on top of hers, then gently pressing his canine teeth against the delicate skin of her neck, began sucking noisily, with Mitsuko's face growing

paler all the while until she suddenly flushed crimson and the beads of sweat standing out on her forehead got sticky from the shock of feeling a thing with both the flexibility and indifference of a vegetable slide into her vagina, but as she writhed, struggling to get away, he flipped her over and, easily grabbing her thighs, one in each hand, raised them up and began licking her rectum, now poised precariously in midair. The sheer size of his tongue, the amount of saliva dripping from it, and the heavy panting were all literally extraordinary. (26–27)

This dizzying description of their sexual intercourse, with one verb following another in rapid succession, can be seen as a parody of the narrative thrust of gothic romance. In conventional gothic fiction, the erotic charge of the narrative often derives from the threat of rape by the wild, mysterious outsider to whom the heroine feels irresistibly attracted. This sexual fear turns into romance toward the end of the story when she finally recognizes his troubled past and his violent passion for her. Tawada's story inverts this pattern by placing the rape scene at the very beginning of their relationship, right after their initial encounter. The vampiric act of sucking the victim's neck is here turned into a doggish expression of affection, and his complete neglect of her breasts—no bodice ripping takes place—and the anticlimactic insertion of his vegetablelike, "indifferent" penis,[12] followed by his dutiful licking of her bottom in a manner evocative of the dog in the folktale, point to the fundamentally unromantic nature of their relationship. Mitsuko seems unintimidated by the mysterious intruder; neither does she feel any special urge to find out about his past. Although they start living together and having sex regularly, their relationship never develops into romance.

Every day, after performing this "canine" sexual ritual, Tarō runs into the kitchen, prepares an exemplary home-cooked meal, "wolf[s] it down," and starts rigorously cleaning Mitsuko's house (28). This self-invited handsome bridegroom, who impeccably performs all the housework for the heroine, parodically mirrors those beautiful and resourceful heroines of traditional tales such as Beauty, Snow White, and the Crane Wife. At the same time, Tarō's overfastidiousness echoes the mothers' obsession with hygiene and decorum, which makes the reader suspect that this doglike Prince Charming may be born out of these romance-seeking housewives' fantasies or at least partly embroidered by them. The reversal of gender roles, however, is not what makes Tawada's retelling radically different from the traditional animal bridegroom story.

In Tawada's story, the transformation works only one way, from humans into dogs. Tarō's habit of smelling Mitsuko's body for over an hour every day begins to make her aware of various subtle nuances of her body aromas changing according to the mood of the moment, so that she gets into the habit of smelling her own body to check her feelings and also starts to feel disturbed by the various chemical smells coming from the mothers. Her newly developed sensitivity to smell seems to indicate the beginning of the process of her transformation into a dog. This possibility becomes more likely when Tarō's history is revealed.

One day, Mrs. Orita, the mother of one of Mitsuko's pupils, recognizes Tarō as her husband's ex-colleague who suddenly disappeared three years ago. According to Mrs. Orita, Tarō used to work for a pharmaceutical company, where he did not quite fit in with the others because of his obsession with cleanliness; the pharmaceutical company can be seen as representing human beings' endeavor to control nature and the body, an endeavor that Tarō seems to have taken too seriously. Mrs. Orita then informs Tarō's wife, Ryōko, about his whereabouts, and Ryōko invites Mitsuko to her flat in a housing complex in a neighboring town that looks exactly like the one where Mitsuko's pupils live. When Mitsuko arrives, Ryōko tells her that she has been "training" to make herself as physically fit as Tarō has become after he left her and, just as Tarō did when he first met Mitsuko, she suddenly lifts Mitsuko's body, lays her flat across the table, and starts sucking her knee, saying, "I feel I'm gradually turning into Taro somehow" (50). Ryōko then tells the story of how Tarō changed completely after being attacked by a pack of stray dogs in the woods. He was taken to a hospital in a police car. His grandmother arrived at the hospital "with wild look in her eye" and uttered a sinister warning: "The boy's lost. An evil spirit's got him now" (52), thus adding a flavor of the werewolf legend to this episode.[13] After this accident, he stopped talking to Ryōko and soon left both her and his job. He was, however, still to be seen in the neighborhood park or station, "each time looking more muscular, with a brighter gleam in his eyes, moving with such agility" (53), a physical state of which she became envious. This apprentice dog-woman, who seems to offer the gothic double to both Tarō and Mitsuko, leaves the story at this point, probably because she is regarded by Mitsuko's pupils and their mothers as irrelevant to their story, being merely an outsider living in the next town. Besides, she does not fit into the stereotype of the jealous and revengeful abandoned wife commonly found in soap operas; she has already started to follow her own path which, exciting and subversive as it seems, does not cross with those of the rest of the characters.

Mitsuko also learns from Ryōko that Tarō has started to "play around" at night with Toshio, the father of the girl Fukiko, who is Mitsuko's favorite pupil (48). Fukiko's name includes the sound *fuku*, the verb "to wipe" in Japanese, indicating her connection with the motif of licking in the folktale. When Mitsuko realizes that Fukiko is bullied by the other children, she asks them why they do it. The children explain that it is because Fukiko is "strange," "fat," "never washes her hair," and sometimes "doesn't even wear socks" (24), indicating their perception of her as someone who deviates from the rules of their clean and civilized community, placing her on the side of the not-quite-human south. Mitsuko feels protective toward this motherless nine-year-old girl, who is left alone in the evenings with enough money to arrange dinner for herself, so she persuades Fukiko to come to her house every day after school and share the dinner Tarō has cooked. Watching this quiet and absentminded girl, "Mitsuko often felt a love akin to irritation well up in her, so strong it hurt" (57). They develop an intimate relationship, echoing the motif of mother-child incest absent in the Japanese and Okinawan variants of the dog bridegroom tale: "[W]hen, for example, Mitsuko took Fukiko's blouse off so she could sew on the buttons that were hanging by a thread, the girl would sit there beside her, naked to the waist, intently watching the movements of her fingers, and after a while her head would be leaning against Mitsuko's shoulder, and when Mitsuko was sure she must have fallen asleep, she'd look over to find the child still gravely following the needle with her eyes"(57–58).

When the children become aware of the special intimacy growing between Mitsuko and Fukiko, they stop bullying Fukiko openly, instead spreading a malicious rumor about her father "'swinging his hips' at the Game Center" with Tarō (58). Although the children seem to be using the expression "swinging his hips" without knowing exactly what it means, the mothers infer that it refers to a homosexual relationship. Hearing this rumor, Mrs. Orita—her name evokes *orime tadashii,* a Japanese phrase meaning being formal and proper—desperately tries to persuade Mitsuko to marry Tarō; Mitsuko, however, has no desire to marry, which itself thwarts any attempt at a conventionally respectable ending. Fukiko's father, who might be expected to play the role of the huntsman who replaces the dog husband in the Japanese variant, is of course no help here, as his desire is clearly oriented toward men. Struggling to make sense of the relationships between those whom they regard as different from themselves, the mothers try to make them fit into some kind of frame they can recognize: heterosexual marriage between Mitsuko and Tarō, and proper family bonds between Fukiko and her father.

At the end of the story, however, all four not-quite-human characters escape from this frame; Tarō disappears with Fukiko's father, and on the same day Mitsuko elopes with Fukiko. It is as if they were conveniently kicked out of the story, banished to somewhere remote—preferably a desert island or the mountains, as in the folktales—when it looked as if they were deviating too far from the conventional pattern. With their disappearance, order is now apparently restored to the community, with the boundary between the human and the nonhuman firmly reestablished: "The house where Mitsuko had lived was soon torn down to make room for some apartments, and by the time construction began, the children were all going to new cram schools, and hardly ever ventured into that part of town again" (62).

This ending, however, conforms to the conventional pattern of stories of interspecies marriage only superficially. In "The Crane Wife," the moment the hero discovers his wife's true animal identity, she disappears. In Tawada's story, on the other hand, the mothers' curiosity as to who Mitsuko and Tarō really are remains ungratified, as none of the four intermediary characters has either revealed his or her true identity in the way the mothers expected or transformed into something that they can identify. Tarō, whom the mothers wish to identify with the dog in the folktale, is shown to be following a completely different plot with his new partner, "each holding a suitcase, standing so close together their bodies touched" (61) as they wait for a train. Spotting Mr. Orita on the opposite platform, Tarō gives his former colleague a polite bow and a word of gratitude for his concern before disappearing into a train, into another story. We are not even told what becomes of the heroine, who leaves the story in the midst of turning into a dog-woman. Like the princess in the desert island version, she is united with her much younger dependent, but it is left to the reader's imagination whether this same-sex union will procreate a new clan as in the origin myth.

As its self-referential title indicates, Tawada's "The Bridegroom Was a Dog" is a variant of the dog bridegroom tale as well as a story *about* this tale type. It shows how certain plot patterns and motifs in traditional tales may generate new variants while at the same time shaping them into recognizable patterns. The conflicted narratives of the mothers reflect their desire to deviate from *and* conform to what they already know. The story, therefore, is also about the difficulty of stepping out of the old patterns without becoming just another variant that does not radically subvert our expectations. Tawada's rewriting structurally departs from traditional narratives by definitively resisting the desire for stability and closure usually fulfilled at the end of the story. The four characters exit the story in the midst of metamorphosis, in a state of fluidity, pregnant with infinite variations.

What is transformed in Tawada's text, instead, is the sense of reality shared by the mothers who build narratives around what they believe to be real, which turns out to be as imaginary as folktales. Amann aptly points out that the distinctive quality of Tawada's rewriting of the tale of metamorphosis lies in its blurring of boundaries between fact and fiction, which "not only problematizes the possibility of giving an accurate account of reality, but also reveals that the 'real' reality itself is a fiction influenced by and constructed from various discourses" (122). Although apparently back to their familiar reality, the children and their mothers in the north of the town will be occasionally haunted by the story of Mitsuko, especially when they are sitting on the toilet.

In this chapter, I have discussed the way in which Tawada uses the motif and structure of animal bride and bridegroom stories in order to reconfigure the notions of various forms of otherness, be it cultural, linguistic, or sexual. The otherness of nonhuman characters remains unresolved throughout the story; rather, it is multiplied through the juxtaposition of different narrative and linguistic conventions. Tawada's "The Bridegroom Was a Dog" self-reflexively plays the noncanonical Asian narrative structures and motifs off against those of the Western and the modern Japanese canon. Also notable is Tawada's play with Chinese characters, which resists transparent translation into those languages that do not use Chinese characters, including her second language, German. Chinese characters in this story can be seen as a metaphor for the kind of otherness that always remains irresolvable yet continues to enchant many people, just as animal partners in fairy tales do.

3

OGAWA YŌKO'S INVITATION
to the BLOODY CHAMBER

Ogawa Yōko's works are often associated with the fairy tale chiefly for their simple, abstract style, eerie atmosphere, and subtly surreal courses of events. Ogawa's use of the abstract fairy-tale mode seems also connected with her sympathy for Kawai Hayao's concepts of archetypal psychology. In my discussion of Ogawa's works, I will also pay attention to the different ways in which they have been received in Japan and in the West. Unlike Tawada, who moves between two cultures and writes in two languages, Ogawa has always been based in Japan, although her works have been appreciated widely in other parts of the world, especially in France. A comparison between the reception of her works in Japan and in the West reveals the still persistent Orientalizing forces operating in today's global circulation of literature. I will suggest a use of fairy-tale criticism for the purpose of re-Orienting such power imbalance.

OGAWA AND THE FAIRY TALE

Ogawa was born in 1962 in Okayama Prefecture in western Japan. After finishing high school, she moved to Tokyo to study creative writing at Waseda University. She had been working as a clerical secretary at a university hospital in her hometown for a couple of years when, in 1988, she won the Kaien Prize for New Writers for her novella based on her graduation project, titled "Agehachō ga kowareru toki" (1988; When a Swallowtail Butterfly Disintegrates). Since then, she has published more than forty works of fiction and nonfiction and has received several major literary awards in Japan, including the Akutagawa Prize for her novella "Ninshin karendā" (1990; "Pregnancy Diary"; English translation, 2005). *Hakase no aishita sūshiki* (2003; translated into English as *The Housekeeper and the Professor* in 2009), her best-selling novel in Japan, won the Yomiuri Prize for Literature and the inaugural Booksellers Award.

Ogawa's novels have also reached a wide audience outside Japan. Most of her fictional works are now available in French translation, and it was through the French versions that her work first came to the attention of English-speaking readers. Her English translator Stephen Snyder claims that she was first received in the English-language publishing world more as a "French" writer than as a Japanese one.[2] Snyder also states that his English translation of Ogawa's work is deeply influenced by the style of her French translator Rose-Marie Makino-Fayolle as well as by the aesthetics and sensibilities of the *New Yorker*'s fiction editor Deborah Treisman, who first commissioned him to translate Ogawa's work, and the other English-speaking editors—mostly female—who were impressed by the French translations of her work. The international circulation of Ogawa's writings, therefore, indicates the growing network of female-oriented writers, readers, and editors across different languages and cultures. The *New Yorker* published abridged versions of her novellas "Yūgure no kyūshokushitsu to ame no pūru" (1991; The Cafeteria in the Evening and a Pool in the Rain) and "Pregnancy Diary" in 2004 and 2005 respectively, which has led to the subsequent book-length publications of English translations of Ogawa's work by Picador.

So far, four books by Ogawa have appeared in English, all translated by Snyder: *The Diving Pool* (2008), a collection of three novellas, "The Diving Pool" ("Daivingu pūru," 1989), "Pregnancy Diary," and "Dormitory" ("Domitorī," 1990), *The Housekeeper and the Professor, The Hotel Iris* (*Hoteru airisu*, 1996; English translation, 2010), and *Revenge: Eleven Dark Tales* (*Kamokuna shigai, midarana tomurai*, 1998; the title literally means "reticent corpse, indecent funeral"; English translation, 2013). *The Diving Pool* won the 2009 Shirley Jackson Award in America, and *The Hotel Iris* was short-listed for the Man Asian Literary Prize in 2010. Three of her novels have been made into films, including *L'annulaire* (2005; The Ring Finger), a film based on her novella "Kusuriyubi no hyōhon" (1992; Specimen of the Ring Finger) and directed by the French Diane Bertrand, which I will discuss in detail later.

One reason Ogawa's work is often associated with the fairy tale lies in its minimalist, non-culture-specific style, which creates an abstract, universal atmosphere characteristic of the fairy tale as described by Max Lüthi in *The European Folktale: Form and Nature* (1947). As in traditional fairy tales, many of her characters do not have names and are known by their professions, social positions, family relationships, or some peculiarities of appearance. None of the main characters of "Pregnancy Diary," for example, has a name; they are called "I," "my sister," and "my brother-in-law" throughout the story. Two of the main characters of *The Housekeeper and the Professor*, as indicated in the title, are called by their professions, and the housekeeper's son, another main character, is called Root, a nickname given by the professor because the shape of his head reminds him of the mathematical symbol $\sqrt{}$. Few places have names, and when they do, only the initials are given, as is the case with "M Clinic" in "Pregnancy Diary" and "F Island" in *Hotel Iris*.

Some of Ogawa's works contain evidently supernatural elements. In "Samenai kōcha" (1990; Tea That Does Not Go Cold), for example, the heroine forms a close friendship with her old classmate from junior high school and his wife, both of whom turn out to have been dead for several years. Even after becoming aware of the possibility that she has been seeing their ghosts, she still visits them in their house, vaguely wondering why the tea her friend makes for her remains hot for such a long time. Equally haunting is *Hisoyakana kesshō* (1994; Secret Crystallization), a novel set on an island where people gradually become deprived both of things around them and of their memories of those objects, including novels—the heroine is a novelist—and even parts of their own bodies.

Most of Ogawa's works, however, hover between reality and fantasy. Her fictional world often seems to float, as it were, just a few centimeters above the everyday world. In her short story "Chūgoku yasai no sodatekata" (2001, How to Grow Chinese Vegetables), for example, the heroine is given the seeds of an obscure vegetable by an old woman and plants them in a pot. The vegetable grows at a disturbing speed and starts to emit a faint yet steady light in her bedroom at night. As the heroine stands spellbound in the darkening street holding a pot of gleaming vegetables at the story's ending, so the reader is left in a state in which the world of everyday reality appears eerily illuminated by Ogawa's "fairy-tale surrealism," to use the American reviewer Ron Charles's words.

Ogawa produces this subtly dislocated sense of reality also by coining words that do not actually exist but at the same time sound intriguingly familiar, inviting the reader to imagine stories behind those words. This technique of combining familiar words in an unfamiliar way in order to produce an uncanny feeling is most evident in her fairy-tale collection *Otogibanashi no wasuremono* (2006; Lost and Found Fairy Tales; figure 3.1). The frame story of this collection is narrated by the librarian of the "Lost and Found Library," which holds fairy tales collected by the narrator's grandfather from lost property offices all over the world.

Included in the Lost and Found Library's collection are four embedded stories based on fairy tales and children's stories widely known in both Western and non-Western cultures: "Little Red Riding Hood," "The Little Mermaid," *Alice's Adventures in Wonderland*, and *Swan Lake*. Higami Kumiko, the illustrator of Matsumoto's fairy-tale collection mentioned in chapter 1, first drew illustrations and then invited Ogawa to write stories inspired by her illustrations.[3]

In "Zukin kurabu" (The Hood Club), Ogawa weaves a story around the word *hood* from "Little Red Riding Hood." The titular club is formed by a group of people obsessed with hoods, an idea that seems not entirely implausible but rather peculiar. The reason the word *hood* triggered the author's imagination may be because it sounds quaint in present-day Japanese when translated as *zukin*, the word used by the early translators of the tale at the end of the nineteenth century that is still customarily used in the translation of "Little Red Riding Hood" but not for much else. The narrator-heroine of the story, who is not a member of the club, meets a hooded woman who introduces herself as the founder and president of the Hood Club. The woman, the heroine soon finds out, makes her living as a seamstress specializing in making new dresses out of old, a craft suggestive of the art of storytelling as well as of the sartorial motif of pins and needles in "The Story of Grandmother," an oral version of "Little Red Riding Hood." The heroine is then invited to the club's annual Hood Festival, in which various aspects of hoods are celebrated. The exhibition includes hoods either made or collected by the members and hood-related artworks.

FIGURE 3.1. Cover of *Otogibanashi no wasuremono*, by Ogawa Yōko. Illustration by Higami Kumiko. Tokyo: HOME-SHA, 2006. Courtesy of HOME-SHA.

The historical, cultural, and political significance of the hood is also explored; one of the slide presentations, for example, is titled "The Effects of the Hood on the Rise of the Female Suffrage Movement." At the climax of the festival, the president makes a speech, wearing what she claims is the "original" red riding hood worn by the heroine of the Grimms' story. The narrator later discovers that the hood is made of the fur of the president's wolf-colored pet dog, apparently sacrificed for her project of materializing the fictional hood from a fairy tale, which the president regards as the most significant hood in Western culture. In Ogawa's rewriting, the word *hood*, taken out of the context of the original tale, triggers a new story, in this case one about a woman who uses a fairy tale to authenticate her sartorial craftsmanship[4] which, in turn, breathes new life into one of the most widely read and most diversely interpreted of tales.

Another story woven around the motif of craftsmanship in *Lost and Found Fairy Tales* is "Ningyo hōseki shokunin" (The Life of a Merman Lapidary), a rewriting of "The Little Mermaid."[5] Ogawa's version is told from the perspective of a merman who makes jewelry for mermaids using underwater materials such as pearls, starfish, and sea grapes. He falls in love with the youngest mermaid princess, for whom he is honored to make a ring to decorate her tail fin. The Little Mermaid, however, falls in love with a human prince and, as in Andersen's story, asks the witch to give her a pair of legs in exchange for her tongue. The prince, however, soon abandons her to marry a human princess. Her mermaid sisters obtain from the witch a magic knife with which the Little Mermaid has to stab the prince in order to regain her mermaid form. As in the original story, however, she chooses to kill herself with the knife. After her death, the merman lapidary carries the ring he made for her to the seashore and dies the moment he is exposed to sunlight. The prince's wife finds the beautiful ring on the shore and wears it around her neck. Then she realizes that she cannot take it off. The ring starts to tighten around her neck and chokes her to death.

Not only do "The Hood Club" and "The Life of a Merman Lapidary" share an emphasis on the transformative power of pursuing one's craft, they also both end with cruel murders committed by the main characters. In both stories, the narrative is delicately crafted toward the final act of cruelty, a latent plot in which the reader also becomes implicated. What is unique about Ogawa's use of the fairy tale lies less in her explicit use of fairy-tale motifs and style than in her more implicit use of dark desires underpinning some of the most widely known fairy tales, especially those with the Forbidden Chamber motif, of which "Bluebeard" is probably the most famous story in the West. In what follows, I will argue how Ogawa's three Bluebeard stories, "Dormitory," "Specimen of the Ring Finger," and *Hotel Iris,* use the Forbidden Chamber motif to explore women's deepest fears and desires.

ON THE THRESHOLD OF THE BLOODY CHAMBER: "DORMITORY" AND "SPECIMEN OF THE RING FINGER"

The motif of Bluebeard first appeared in Ogawa's work in "Dormitory," one of her early novellas, included in her first collection in English, *The Diving Pool.* In this story, a recently married woman, lonely and bored during her husband's absence, becomes drawn toward an old dormitory inhabited only by a mysterious crippled caretaker. The story begins when she starts experiencing "a quaking, a current, even a throb" that triggers the memory of her old college dormitory: "There is a place in my memory that is dim and obscure, and the sound seems to have been hiding just there" (109–10). Here, it is indicated that the Forbidden Chamber, from which the mysterious sound seems to issue, is located within herself, the "dim and obscure" part of her own psyche. In the midst of preparing to move to Sweden, where her husband is now settled, she has nothing else to do but patchwork during the day and watch television in the evening; she feels that her life is "drifting in circles": "Formless days passed one after the other, as if swollen into an indistinguishable mass by the damp weather" (117). Her life brightens up when she receives a phone call from her cousin, who is about to start his university career in Tokyo and who wants to rent a room in the same dormitory that she left six years ago. When she revisits the dormitory with her cousin, she finds it empty except for the caretaker, an aging man missing one leg and both arms. As her cousin fills out the application form, they watch him making tea for them, deftly manipulating the materials with his chin, collarbone, and one leg.

She frequently attempts to visit her cousin in the dormitory, but whenever she comes she is told that he is not in, so each time she ends up chatting with the caretaker over a cup of tea. She feels uneasy when he passionately praises her cousin's body parts: "I can assure you he has a marvellous body—perfect for team handball. Strong fingers to grip that ball, a flexible spine for the jump shot, long arms for blocking, powerful shoulders for the long pass" (136). She learns from him about a first-year math student who suddenly disappeared without leaving any trace. She is again upset by the caretaker's outburst of praise for that young man's fingers, which he liked to watch while the student planted tulip bulbs: "I couldn't take my eyes off of the beautiful fingers on his left hand. . . . The fingers were pale and slender—like exotic hothouse flowers. But each part seemed to have its own expressive quality—as if the nail on the ring finger could smile, or the joint of the thumb was shy" (145).

The heroine becomes more and more drawn toward the dormitory, which seems to suffer from the same self-afflicting decay as that eroding the caretaker's body; his ribs, he tells her, are gradually caving inward and affecting his heart and lungs. One day, while attending to the now bedridden caretaker, she notices thick, sticky liquid dripping down from the ceiling just above his bed. As more and more drops start to fall, even onto her body, all the mysteries suddenly come together: "The boy who solved math problems with a pencil, who planted bulbs with a tiny shovel—where had he gone? Drip. Why were the tulips such strange colors? Drop. Where was my cousin? Drip. How did the Manager know so much about my cousin's joints and muscles?" (161). She immediately rushes upstairs to break into the space above his room to find the source of the dripping liquid. There, she finds not the bodies of young men but an enormous beehive: "It had grown so huge that it had begun to split open in places, and honey spilled from the cracks, dripping slowly and thickly, just like blood" (164).

In "Dormitory," the heroine's loneliness and her inner anxieties about going abroad to join her husband drive her to revisit the dormitory where she spent her youth, only to find that the dormitory is no longer the same but is shadowed by loss, decay, and death. The Bluebeard figure in this story compensates for the lost parts of his own body by ruminating over the beautiful body parts of ever-absent young men. Driven not by curiosity but by a more urgent need to find out the truth, the heroine decides to unlock the Forbidden Chamber and discovers an accumulation of her anxieties and desires, symbolized by the monstrous beehive oozing honey. The story ends there: the protagonist, rather than frozen with fear like the heroine of Perrault's story, reaches out to the hive, suggesting her reconciliation with the part of her psyche that has been unresolved and that has resurged in her imprisonment as a housewife.

"Dormitory," therefore, can be interpreted as a female-centered retelling of "Bluebeard." However, no criticism has so far engaged with this intertextual reading. In the case of Japanese readers, this oversight comes partly from the marginalized status of "Bluebeard" in the Japanese canon of European fairy tales, compared to such tales as "Cinderella," "Snow White," and "Little Red Riding Hood," which have played a significant role in the modernization of Japanese culture, as I discussed in chapter 1. It also reflects the lack of interest in feminist fairy-tale criticism in Japanese literary studies. In the case of Western critics, on the other hand, the absence of overtly sexual content in Ogawa's story may have deflected their attention from its use of the Bluebeard motif. Interestingly, when Ogawa returned to the Bluebeard motif in "The Specimen of the Ring Finger," although Japanese critics continued to ignore the fairy-tale intertext, the French film director Diane Bertrand saw the connection between Ogawa's story and "Bluebeard" and expanded on this intertextual potential by resexualizing the story.

Ogawa's "Specimen of the Ring Finger" is narrated by a young woman who leaves her job after losing the tip of her ring finger in a factory accident. She becomes an assistant to a technician specializing in making, with the use of preservative fluid, everlasting "specimens" of objects that his clients wish to preserve because of important memories associated with them. She then hears a rumor that his previous female assistants mysteriously disappeared after going into his laboratory in the basement, to which he has forbidden her entry. She eventually decides to have her wounded ring finger made into a specimen, knowing that the technician's preservation method does not allow a body part to be separated from the whole body—thus, her whole body will be turned into a specimen in formaldehyde.

Critics in Japan tend to read this story as a kind of biotechnological gothic fiction and focus on the way it depicts the body as devoid of substance—the body fetishized and made into specimen, a metaphor especially apt for the age of virtual reality (Fuse 184). This tale, however, can be interpreted as the story of the girl's discovery of her body through her relationship with the mysterious man who seems to hold the key to the secret of the body. This implication becomes clearer when we recognize the plot pattern of "Bluebeard." Just before she knocks on the door of the laboratory, the heroine dreams of the sensuous pleasure of being immersed in warm liquid inside a test tube, quietly looking out into the technician's eyes.

It is interesting that, whereas Ogawa's story ends when the heroine knocks on the door of the secret laboratory, Bertrand's film adaptation ends just as the door opens to reveal a space filled with light—suggesting, surprisingly, in contrast to the usual interpretation of "Bluebeard," the heroine's liberation rather than her death (figure 3.2). The film also fore-grounds the heroine's sexual relationship with the technician and adds another relationship—with a young man working in the dockyard—that does not appear in the original story. This liaison develops alongside her relationship with the technician, but in the end she decides to abandon it. The film, therefore, brings the theme of sexual curiosity to the fore, rendering explicit the Bluebeard motif latent in Ogawa's story, whose fairy-tale plot, again, has failed to attract Japanese readers' attention. It is interesting that "Bluebeard," a familiar fairy tale from Bertrand's own culture, seems to have helped Bertrand understand this ambiguous story by the Japanese writer who apparently did not have this particular fairy tale in her mind when she wrote it. This shows how traditional fairy tales can work as an interpretive framework for readers across different cul-tures, inspiring new intertexual and intercultural readings and retellings which, in turn, will complicate our understanding of the "original" stories.

Thus, reading Ogawa's works from the perspective of feminist fairy-tale criticism can reveal a dimension that may go unnoticed if they remain within the context of a culture-specific literary tradition. In what follows,

FIGURE 3.2. *L'annulaire*. Directed by Diane Bertrand. 2005.

I will first consider the implications of the contrasting receptions of Ogawa's novel *Hotel Iris* in Japan and in the West. I will then interpret *Hotel Iris* as a more radical recasting of "Bluebeard" than her previous works.

A JAPANESE BLUEBEARD? *HOTEL IRIS* IN A GLOBAL CONTEXT

In *Hotel Iris,* a beautiful, fatherless girl is drawn to a much older man who lives on an almost deserted island and who is rumored to have murdered his wife.[6] Their relationship is cut off by the girl's "rescue," instigated by her mother, an intervention that also results in her lover's death. Although there is no explicit reference to "Bluebeard," the novel can be read as an adaptation of the fairy tale set in present-day Japan.[7]

The most disturbing figure in this story is not the mysterious man but the heroine herself, who retrospectively narrates their sadomasochistic relationship with a calm, observant eye; it soon becomes clear to the reader that she takes pleasure in her own suffering and fantasizes about becoming his next murdered wife. In the context of Western feminist fairy-tale rewritings and criticism, which have emphasized the socioeconomic basis of Bluebeard's attractions for underprivileged girls—most notably Angela Carter's "The Bloody Chamber" and the critical discourse around it[8]—the heroine's active pursuit of masochistic desire may appear to be an uncritical embrace of an old patriarchal plot. It is true that Ogawa is writing in a cultural context where women's sexual masochism is a common topos in pornography and where feminist criticism is still marginalized compared to the West: Carter's observation forty years ago that "Japan is a man's country" still holds true in many ways (*Fireworks* 6). Against this critical grain, however, I will try to show how a cross-cultural analysis of *Hotel Iris* reveals a new dimension of the Bluebeard story that can be reworked for a feminist purpose.

Before going into the textual analysis of *Hotel Iris,* I will first consider the novel's reception in a global context. From a cross-cultural perspective, it is interesting that, although *Hotel Iris* is Ogawa's most widely translated work (translated into nine languages), it has not been regarded as one of her major works in Japan. The Japanese critic Ayame Hiroharu's description of the novel as "adventurous" and "experimental," terms that he uses here as euphemisms for failure, seems to typify its general evaluation in

Japan (122). On the other hand, in France, where most of her novels have been translated, *Hotel Iris* is one of her most popular works, and it is her only work short-listed for the Man Asian Literary Prize, an award given to a novel by an Asian writer that is either written in English or translated into English. The Australian writer Stephanie Bishop claims in her review of *Hotel Iris,* titled "Besotted with Pain," that, among the three books by Ogawa available in English translation (*Revenge* had not yet appeared at the time), "*Hotel Iris* is her best performance yet." Where does this disparity in reception between domestic and Western reviewers come from?

This line of inquiry is useful when considering the changing constellation of today's global literary cultures. The disparity in the reception and interpretation of *Hotel Iris* between Japan and the West seems to exemplify the different effects a literary work may have when it travels beyond its cultural and linguistic origin. As David Damrosch argues, a literary work may "gain in translation" in this process of recontextualization (*What Is World Literature?* 281). At the same time, a translated work may affect the literary climate of another culture, remapping the genre's tradition. As I will argue below, *Hotel Iris* offers an example of this mode of literary cross-fertilization when it enters into a new critical dialogue informed by feminist fairy-tale studies in the West.

The most conspicuous interpretative difference in the reception of *Hotel Iris* may be that Japanese critics tend to focus on the novel's controversial subject matter—the sadomasochistic relationship between a young girl and an old man—whereas Western reviewers lay more emphasis on the style of Ogawa's prose and the atmosphere it creates, which they describe as "eerie," "dreamlike," "glassy," and "economical," adjectives often associated with the style of the fairy tale. Japanese reviews usually quote the most sexually explicit scenes and find Ogawa's style and sensibility unsuitable—too ladylike is often the implied criticism—for telling a story of sexual transgression. For Western reviewers, on the other hand, it seems as if the novel could be enjoyed for its style even *despite* its story. Bishop writes: "If the story is at times repellent, the writing is always compelling." But are they reading the same story?

At least two English-language reviews associate *Hotel Iris* with "Bluebeard"; one of these is titled "Bluebeard in Japan."[9] On the other hand, there has been no mention of "Bluebeard" in Japanese reviews and criticisms of *Hotel Iris*. As I pointed out earlier, this omission results from the marginality of both "Bluebeard" and feminist fairy-tale criticism in Japan. Instead, the most frequent intertextual reference noted by its Japanese readers is Vladimir Nabokov's *Lolita*, whose subject matter has been so highly fetishized that its title has entered Japanese vocabulary as *Lolicon*, an abbreviation of the phrase "Lolita complex," referring to a widespread subcultural phenomenon of men's sexual attraction to prepubescent and pubescent girls. As Maria Tatar argues in *Secrets beyond the Door: The Story of Bluebeard and His Wives* (2004), *Lolita* can be read as a Bluebeard story about a man who keeps a secret diary hidden in a locked drawer (153–56), which suggests that the Japanese and Western reviewers *are* reading the same story. However, the significant difference between *Lolita* and "Bluebeard" is that the former is narrated from the male protagonist's point of view whereas the latter is more geared toward the female experience. It is no wonder that the heroine of *Hotel Iris* is not interested in the elevation of an aging pervert to an aesthetic hero or a Prince Charming, a status for which, Tatar argues, Humbert Humbert strives through his writing. To read *Hotel Iris* as *Lolita* which, in the Japanese cultural context, denotes men's sexual fantasy about young girls, is to overlook its female-centered perspective and plot; this *mis*reading by Japanese (male) readers indicates the predominance of the misogynistic Lolicon phenomenon, which has eclipsed "Bluebeard" in Japanese culture.[10] Although some may see *Hotel Iris* as a reverse version of *Lolita*,[11] this reading still misses the main plot of Ogawa's novel. What connects the two novels seems to be more to do with their style than their content; in both, it is the power of language that seduces the reader into following the narrator-protagonist's quest for love, however deranged and disturbing the project itself may be.

In the context of modern Japanese fiction, *Hotel Iris* can be associated with Kawabata Yasunari's "House of the Sleeping Beauties." *Hotel Iris* uses a restrained narrative voice evocative of that of Kawabata, a voice that makes a striking contrast with the disturbing subject matter, while reversing the gender of the narrator. Despite its title, however, Kawabata's story, told from the perspective of a man obsessed with inert underage girls, resembles Nabokov's *Lolita* more closely than "Sleeping Beauty," a fairy tale that, like "Bluebeard," is focused on a female experience. Another intertextual reference generally overlooked by both Japanese and

Western readers is Tanizaki Jun'ichirō's work, which often employs masochism as a key transcendental aesthetic force. His *Shunkin shō* (1933; A Portrait of Shunkin), for example, reaches the moment of aesthetic sublimation when the protagonist willingly pierces his own eyes with a needle in a self-sacrificing act of love for his domineering female music teacher. Mishima Yukio's semiautobiographical novel *Kamen no kokuhaku* (1949; *Confessions of a Mask*) also deals with the male protagonist's masochistic desire to suffer and die like Saint Sebastian. Ogawa's novel, therefore, can be seen as a feminist repurposing of the "confessions of a male masochist" tradition in Japanese literature, reversing the gender roles assumed in the male predecessors' works, which posit the woman as a static point of reference rather than as a subject capable of transformation.

While these culture-specific intertextual connections need to be taken into consideration in an analysis of *Hotel Iris,* it is also important to note the way in which its cultural ambiguity appeals to different audiences. In an essay about the effects of travel on her writing, Ogawa remarks that *Hotel Iris* was inspired by the atmospheric fort standing on a tidal island in Saint-Malo, a town with "timber-framed houses that may appear in fairy tales, high stone castle walls surrounding them, the main street lined with fashionable French restaurants, and the seashore, which seems to extend endlessly" (*Fukaki kokoro no soko yori* 189).[12] Ogawa further explains that, although her original plan was to write a story set in France, her childhood memory of the boat trips she used to make near her hometown—"even though they were so small, they meant an escape from everyday life" (191)—took over and became superimposed on her romanticized image of the French coast, which she visited as an adult. This in-betweenness, between the provincial Japanese town of her childhood memory and the remote, romanticized European town, between the present and the past, and between reality and fantasy, gives this fundamentally realistic novel a sense of estrangement from reality, which also characterizes "Bluebeard." Although Perrault's text does not specify where the story is set, "Bluebeard" has been conventionally illustrated as an Oriental story in the style of *The Arabian Nights,* as is the case with influential Victorian illustrations such as those by Gustave Doré and Arthur Rackham.

The main characters of Ogawa's novel are also rendered culturally ambiguous. All the characters and places in the novel are unnamed except for the heroine and the hotel where she lives and works, creating an abstract, fairy-tale-like narrative space. Although Japanese names are usually written in Chinese characters, the heroine's name, Mari, is written in *katakana*, a form of syllabic writing primarily used for transliterating words of foreign origin, thereby giving foreign overtones to her name. Mari's lover, referred to as "the translator" throughout the novel, tells her that the heroine of a Russian novel that he has been translating is also called Marie and that the two are very similar despite their different ethnic and cultural backgrounds. The translator himself is also characterized by cultural duality as someone who makes his living by going back and forth between two languages. That he is always overdressed in a Western suit in a provincial town even in the sweltering heat of subtropical summer gives him an air of an old-fashioned European gentleman, in addition to that of a paranoiac who has lost touch with reality. It is in this symbolic and culturally ambiguous mode that *Hotel Iris* retells the Bluebeard story.

INSIDE THE BLOODY CHAMBER

In *Hotel Iris*, the heroine not only enters the bloody chamber of her own accord, she also willingly participates in Bluebeard's secret rituals. Mari is a seventeen-year-old girl who spends all day working at the shabby seaside hotel owned by her mother—serving breakfast, cleaning rooms, and sitting behind the front desk till late at night. She has no friends and shows no interest in the outside world or even in her own life. Her father died when she was eight, and she lives in the dark back rooms of the hotel with her mother, who treats her in an unreasonably harsh manner and often punishes her by not allowing her to have dinner. She even forced her daughter to quit high school to work at the hotel. At the same time, she extols her daughter's beauty while forcefully taming her hair into a tight bun in front of a mirror every morning in a way that mixes sadism with displaced self-love. The heroine's mother, therefore, can be seen as a fairy-tale stepmother who represents the destructive side of the mother. It is also significant that her mother is tainted with the sexist ideology that objectifies young women; when a drunken customer molests the heroine by grabbing her breasts, the mother scolds her for making a fuss over such a trifle. Mari, like Cinderella, is also harassed by the maid who, like an evil sister in a fairy tale, envies her, steals her small belongings and,

later in the story, tries to prevent her from seeing her lover. The heroine awakens from her Sleeping Beauty–like stupor when, one night, she
hears the deep, commanding voice of an old man who is having a quar-
rel with a prostitute in one of the rooms of the hotel. His commanding
words, "Shut up, whore" (3), penetrate to the bottom of her deeply buried
desires. Some days later, she follows him through the town until he turns
around to confront her. It is she who chooses him, not vice versa.

In the Bluebeard story, the heroine is usually attracted to her wealthy
suitor despite his horrifying blue beard. Ogawa's heroine, however, is aware
from the start that the man is not rich and is captivated by his physical repulsiveness. While talking with him for the first time, she observes
his aging body: "That was the first time I realised that the shape of an
ear changes with age. His was no more than a limp sliver of dark flesh"
(14). Such signs of decay in his body seem to bring her closer to what her
mother—who sees her daughter as representing the part of herself that
is young, beautiful, and innocent—wants to keep away from her. This
Bluebeard-like man mirrors her mother in his role as the one who gives
orders and doles out punishment, and this is where his most powerful
attraction for the heroine lies. There is a torture scene that grotesquely parodies her Cinderella-like enslavement by her mother: she is ordered by her
lover to do household chores naked, holding plates in her mouth and stag-
gering across the room with a heavy chair strapped to her back. After such
scenes of abuse, he tells her how beautiful she is, echoing her mother as
well as the voice of the magic mirror in "Snow White." His profession as a
translator also answers her needs. She says to him: "I think it's wonderful—
helping people understand things they could never know otherwise!" (25).
As she implies here, his role is to translate her as yet undefined desire into
a language she can recognize, giving her the key to the forbidden part of
her psyche. Her need to create a fantasy world to elude suffocating reality
intersects with the old widower's self-imposed estrangement from life.

The fantasy world that this unlikely couple creates together resembles more a gothic horror story than a fairy-tale romance because it is
based on a revenge plot on both sides. On Mari's part, it arises from
her conflicting feelings toward her mother, and her social and emotional
ignorance limits her recourse in working through her impulses to relying
on the same frame of reference, that is, a dominance-submission pattern, and perverting it in such a way that she abuses her own body to

gain control of her life. After her first visit to the translator's house, Mari tries to fix her disarranged hair as neatly as her mother does, but when she returns home, her mother, like Bluebeard noticing the bloodstain on the key, immediately detects aberration and asks: "What have you done to your hair?" (55). While her mother is redoing her hair, Mari enjoys her secret triumph: "I had gone somewhere far away today. Far away over the sea, a place she could never reach. . . . In my heart, I told her that her pretty little Mari had become the ugliest person in the whole world" (57). When her wish to be loved is fulfilled in her sadomasochistic sexual relationship with a stranger, she becomes aware of her complicity in her own incarceration and tries to start telling her own story, albeit in a mimetic way. The Bluebeard figure, despite his sexual knowledge, functions only as a prop in her psychodrama as he is shown to be totally incapable of extricating himself from his own compulsive pattern of behavior.

His sadistic behavior with women and his inability to control his temper in general are explained as symptoms of post-traumatic stress disorder. Mari learns from his nephew, whom she meets later, that, contrary to the rumors, his wife was not murdered by him but died in a railway accident: as she was standing on a platform holding her sister's baby, who is the nephew himself, her scarf got caught between the doors of a departing train, which dragged her body till her head smashed against a pole. Her husband ran shouting for her to save herself by dropping the baby and untying her scarf, which she heroically refused to do. This tragic accident is translated in his mind into the following dictum: his wife died because she did not obey his orders. The motif of a disobedient wife punished with death is given a strange twist in this story; here, Bluebeard is a death-driven man seized by a compulsion to reenact the death of his beloved wife, which was caused by his own powerlessness. While being hung from the ceiling and whipped with a riding crop in the dark pantry of his house, Mari joins his dead wife in her imagination: "My wrists seemed about to rip from my arms, and I pictured the scene to myself. . . . I would fall to the floor. . . . Thick drops fall from above, and when I look up, the head of the translator's wife is hanging from the hook—with the scarf still wrapped around her neck" (151).

Like Bluebeard handing his wife the key to the secret chamber, the translator provides Mari with his own version of the Bluebeard story, which will work as the master narrative for their relationship. This novel within a novel, which he says he is translating from the Russian, tells the story of a woman, conveniently named Marie, who is cruelly persecuted by her husband for her infidelity. He then introduces his nephew, an architecture student and also a painter, to Mari. The nephew is the exact opposite of the translator; he is young, beautiful, and gentle. He has no voice to command as he literally lost his tongue as a result of a disease when he was a child. This character, recalling the figure of the voiceless Little Mermaid, may be expected to act as an antidote to Bluebeard, as the blind piano tuner does in Carter's "The Bloody Chamber." Mari, however, considers him mainly as an obstacle and even as a rival in her relationship with the translator. Nevertheless, she follows the master narrative by seducing the young man precisely in order to be punished by her lover.

The translator punishes her infidelity not by beheading her but by cutting off all her hair, which she describes as a "superb penalty" as it destroys the token of her mother's domination over her (155). Cutting off her beautiful long hair, a motif that also appears in "The Little Mermaid," is also significant in that it is meant to spoil her beauty by destroying the sign of femininity. With her hair unevenly hacked off, she looks like "a chick with bedraggled feathers," grotesquely echoing the heroine of "Fitcher's Bird" (KHM 46), the Grimms' version of "Bluebeard," who disguises herself as a bird by dipping her body in honey and rolling in feathers in order to escape her murderous bridegroom. When Mari returns to the town, it is her hair that works as a telltale proof of her abuse.

On the return boat after this punishment, Mari sees the whole town, including a police car and an ambulance, gathered on the dock and anxiously looking up at the boat. She feels "very strange" when she hears her mother screaming her name in a melodramatic way in what her mother believes to be her daughter's rescue scene (161). Unlike the heroine in "The Bloody Chamber," Mari does not establish female solidarity with her mother at the end of the story. Neither does the story take a romantic turn and follow the marriage plot of stories such as "Cinderella" and "Sleeping Beauty," with which Carter's story merges toward the end when the heroine marries a more suitable man and is promised a happily-ever-after. The translator, pursued by two young men along the deck of the boat, jumps overboard to drown rather than be arrested.

Although the translator's intention is not made clear, his suicide protects Mari from suffering dishonor in a way not dissimilar to that of the Little Mermaid, who also throws herself from the ship into the sea for the sake of her beloved's happiness. After his death, Mari feigns partial amnesia about what happened in his island house and lets the police and the townspeople regard him as a mean pervert who abused an innocent girl. By keeping the secret locked in her mind, she herself becomes Bluebeard, giving the final twist to the motif of the possession of a secret as power in the Bluebeard story. On one level, this outcome can be seen as the daughter's victory over her mother; her mother stops torturing her by pulling her hair and no longer insists on her sitting behind the front desk. On another level, however, it is not certain what kind of story of her own the heroine can start telling now that the old framework of "Bluebeard" has proved illusory; after her lover's death, she finds out that his translation of the Russian novel about Marie does not in fact exist. The cruelest aspect of this ending may be that Mari must now go back to drab reality, that she neither magically transforms into a princess nor turns into the foam of the sea like the Little Mermaid. This ending, therefore, is more ambiguous than reassuring.

On the other hand, the couple's separation at the end of the story is typical of traditional Japanese fairy tales. As I mentioned in my discussion of Tawada's work, Japanese tales are often not marriage oriented, and when they are, as in the case of animal bride and bridegroom tales, they tend to end with a separation, which is accepted as a natural and aesthetic necessity. It is probably for this reason that most of the widely disseminated Japanese translations of Andersen's "The Little Mermaid" cut out the final scene in which the heroine ascends to the kingdom of heaven. Within this cultural context, the final separation of the couple completes an aesthetically satisfying narrative effect rather than being perceived as abrupt or merely tragic. Therefore, it can be said that the ending of *Hotel Iris* redirects the romantic trajectory of the Western fairy tale to merge into this different narrative tradition. This cultural difference in narrative expectation may explain, at least partly, some Western readers' dissatisfaction with the ending of *Hotel Iris;* one American review comments that "a sorrowful and artful ending wraps up the girl's story, though not neatly" (Rev. of *Hotel Iris*). It is telling that Stephen Snyder changed the order of the last two paragraphs in his translation, apparently in an attempt to give the novel the neatest possible ending. Whereas the English translation concludes when the heroine learns from the police that the translation of the Russian novel does not actually exist and that "[a]ll they found were endless rolls of film filled with pictures of me" (164), the Japanese original ends by noting that the nephew never reappeared, a piece of information apparently peripheral to the novel's main plot.

Hotel Iris does not indeed offer any clear-cut feminist solution, but it certainly calls into question the conventional happy ending of "Bluebeard," which can be interpreted as the heroine's regression to her psychological dependence on her family. The novel's use of "Bluebeard" as a narrative framework for working through the girl's emotional struggle with her mother and for mapping out her way toward self-knowledge complicates the psychodynamics of this tale.

In this chapter, I have analyzed Ogawa's stories as feminist reworkings of the Forbidden Chamber motif. Both "Dormitory" and "Specimen of the Ring Finger" follow through the heroines' growing desire to delve below their conscious perception of the body and the mind to the moment when they make a decision to open the door of the Forbidden Chamber. Unlike the traditional Bluebeard story, their final act of transgression does not seem to lead to their persecution; rather, as Bertrand's cross-cultural film adaptation suggests, it opens up a realm of new perceptions, radiating dazzling light. The heroine of *Hotel Iris* takes a step further into the bloody chamber and acts out her secret scenario of her rebellion against her mother. Neither do Ogawa's Bluebeard stories evoke the sense of *aware* often produced at the end of Japanese tales as pointed out by Kawai; rather, they pervert the aestheticization of female self-sacrifice to the heroines' own ends.

On the one hand, the analytical framework of Western feminist fairy-tale criticism helps unpack the subtle yet radical feminist implications of Ogawa's stories. On the other hand, Ogawa's re-Orienting of the Forbidden Chamber motif in a culture where both feminism and the fairy tale have taken different courses of development from the West can illuminate hitherto unexplored aspects of the traditional Western fairy tale.

In my discussion of the different receptions of Ogawa's works in Japan and in the West, I have also pointed out the working of the power imbalance in global literary circulation, arguing that it needs to be taken into consideration in order to avoid colluding with the re-Orientalizing tendency, which may obstruct a deeper, mutually illuminating insight into works produced in non-Western cultures.

4

YANAGI MIWA'S DISMANTLING *of* GRANDMOTHER'S HOUSE

The work of the artist Yanagi Miwa explores received images of women and their own self-images in contemporary Japan. Among the cultural stereotypes she restages in her synthetic photographs and video installations are the images of both young and old female characters in traditional fairy tales such as "Snow White," "Sleeping Beauty," and "Frau Trude." Her fairy-tale images reverse, blend, and dissolve the binary oppositions well established in traditional European tales, often typified by the opposition between the princess and the witch. Yanagi's reconfiguration of the relationship between the young girl and the old woman is more ambiguous than simply either antagonistic or harmonious, an approach that calls into question the assumed naturalness of familiar fairy-tale scenes. These ambiguous images of women, who are at once young and old, beautiful and ugly, and good and evil, can be related to the figure of the yamauba, who appears in various forms in Japanese folklore. In this chapter, I will examine the ways in which Yanagi's work dismantles not only the gender and age stereotypes in traditional fairy tales but also the quintessential storytelling space of the fireside—a symbol of home and family life—to which women and children have traditionally been confined in a patriarchal society.

PERFORMING GENDER AND AGE:
FROM ELEVATOR GIRLS TO MY GRANDMOTHERS

Yanagi was born in Kobe in western Japan in 1967. After finishing her graduate studies in textile art at Kyoto City University of Arts, she initially created abstract installation works using textiles. She then started to produce performance pieces featuring elevator girls at department stores, which developed into her first photographic series, Elevator Girl (1994–99). The Elevator Girl series was followed by her two other major photographic series, My Grandmothers (1999–) and Fairy Tale (2004–6) as well as by several video installations including *Granddaughters* (2004) and *Lullaby* (2010). She was commissioned to represent Japan at the 2009 Venice Biennale, where she exhibited her photographic work and a video installation under the theme Wind Swept Women: Old Girls' Troup. Since 2010, she has been concentrating mainly on theater direction, producing a series of dramatic works titled 1924, in which the motif of women in uniform, recalling her Elevator Girls series, recurs.

Since her first solo exhibition in Kyoto in 1993, her work has been exhibited both in Japan and abroad. That her work has been recognized at home and overseas almost simultaneously seems to have affected the way in which she perceives and represents her own culture in a global context. She has held solo exhibitions at Deutsche Guggenheim, Berlin (2004), Hara Museum of Contemporary Art, Tokyo (2005), Yūrinsō, Ōhara Museum of Art, Okayama (2005), Chelsea Art Museum, New York (2007), the Museum of Fine Arts, Houston, Texas (2008), Tokyo Metropolitan Museum of Photography (2009), and the National Museum of Art, Osaka (2009), among others. She has received several domestic and international awards, including the 1998 Leopold Godowsky Jr. Color Photography Award (Photographic Resource Center at Boston University) and the 1999 VOCA (the Vision of Contemporary Art) Prize (Ueno Royal Museum, Tokyo).

Yanagi's work was first introduced to a Western audience in Prospect '96, a group exhibition held at Schirn Kunsthalle Frankfurt in 1996, which showed her photography along with works by Western artists such as Cindy Sherman and Sam Taylor-Wood as well as work by other Japanese artists who had already established an international reputation, including Morimura Yasumasa (1951–) and Araki Nobuyoshi (1940–). This group exhibition in Germany played a pivotal role in Yanagi's artistic career by giving her the opportunity to sell her work for the first time; as Yanagi states in an interview, there was "no contemporary art market in Japan" at the time, and the concept of a commercial art gallery, as opposed to a rental gallery that charges a rental fee to artists exhibiting their work, was virtually unknown ("Miwa Yanagi"). Getting an opportunity to exhibit overseas, therefore, has had a transformative effect on contemporary Japanese artists by enabling them to make a living as artists while being based in Japan, a situation that grounds their works in a different social and cultural context from the one in which the works of their predecessors used to be placed; Japan-born artists such as Léonard Foujita (Fujita Tsuguharu) (1886–68), Kusama Yayoi (1929–), and Yoko Ono (1933–) became internationally established while living in Western countries.

Yanagi's work is deeply rooted in her experience of living as a woman in Japanese society. Her first major series, Elevator Girls, appeared in the aftermath of the bursting of the bubble economy in Japan. Although the profession referred to as *erebētā-gāru* (elevator girl) had virtually disappeared from Japanese department stores by the end of the 1990s,[1] it had been one of the most sought-after professions for young Japanese women for over half a century, probably ranked just below a flight attendant, which still remains a much-desired job. Apart from pressing the elevator buttons for their customers, elevator girls announce such information as whether the elevator is going up or down and what kind of products can be found on each floor. The superfluous nature of this work seems essential for its fetishized status, which turns young women into a kind of luxury commodity to be viewed for pleasure.

In the Elevator Girls series (figure 4.1), young women of "standard" body proportions wear the same uniform (often in bright red), makeup, and hairstyle and assume an identical expression and similar postures. The provisional nature of their existence—elevator girls are replaced as soon as they are past their bloom, that is, their early twenties—is reflected in the exaggeratedly postmodern settings, which seem to expand endlessly but, in real life, are places we pass through only in transit. In other words, the temporality of commodifiable womanhood is transposed to spatial metaphors indicating passage, such as elevators, escalators, and station platforms. In this series, uniformed and standardized young women are represented both as products of a male-oriented consumer society and as symbols of the image of ideal femininity that can be purchased in places like department stores. These young women look as vacant and lifeless as shop-window mannequins. Yanagi's elevator girls embody a late twentieth-century Japanese version of Snow White in the glass coffin, wearing the color of the poisoned apple that put them out of action and dreaming their standardized, endlessly reproducible dreams behind shop windows.

Yanagi's elevator girls in a way reflect the artist's own self-image, as she herself states in an interview: "The Elevator Girls series was about myself as well as other Japanese women. When I started the series, I

FIGURE 4.1. Yanagi Miwa, *Elevator Girl House 1F* (detail), 1997. 2,400 x 2,000 mm. Chromogenic print. © Miwa Yanagi. Courtesy of the artist.

was working as a teacher after graduating from university. Back then, I strongly felt that I was just playing a role in a standardized society, having a particular occupation in a particular setting. I did not work as an elevator girl literally, but the idea resonated in me in a symbolic way" ("Miwa Yanagi"). In the same interview, however, Yanagi also stresses that feeling "uncomfortable" and "different" in her social environment gives her an impetus to artistic creation. Her work, therefore, expresses both a sense of solidarity with and a detached commentary on women living in contemporary Japan.

This ambivalent attitude toward the subject matter is reflected in the style of her work. All the images in her oeuvre are elaborately manipulated to enhance their constructed nature; as Linda Nochlin puts it, "revealing the device" is her prime strategy (232). This self-reflexivity connects her work not only with Judith Butler's performative theory of gender, a concept that exposes the performative nature of gender identity and that underlies the feminist deconstructionist strategy employed by such artists as Cindy Sherman, but also with the performance of gender in Japanese theater traditions. In Kabuki, a form of traditional Japanese drama, female parts are played by *onnagata* (literally "female form"), male actors who impersonate women not through verisimilitude but with highly stylized gestures and appearance designating the idea of femininity. The reversal of this cross-sexual performance is found in the Takarazuka Revue, an all-female musical theater established in the early twentieth century, in which women play the parts of men in an emphatically stylized form, representing the idealized notion of masculinity for a predominantly female audience. Drawing upon both postmodern aesthetics and Japanese theater traditions, Yanagi's staged and computer-manipulated photographs foreground the performative aspect of identity construction, especially in terms of gender.

At the same time, Yanagi's puppetlike elevator girls also recall Olympia, the life-size automaton in "The Sandman" (1816), a dark *Kunstmärchen* by E. T. A. Hoffmann. In his 1919 essay "The 'Uncanny,'" Freud uses Hoffmann's story to explain the uncanny, an aesthetic phenomenon that he defines as a shade of anxiety caused by the return of what is familiar *and* repressed either in real life or in art. Olympia is a "beautiful, but strangely silent and motionless" girl whom the main character Nathaniel falls violently in love with but who turns out to be an elaborate automaton (137).

Yanagi's Elevator Girls series creates the effect of uncanniness through the ambiguity of its representation of animate and inanimate—the dolls that turn out to be real women—as well as the repetition of the same— the girls as replicas of each other and the architecture endlessly mirroring itself. By exaggerating the standardized, impassive beauty of young women and the surrounding space, the Elevator Girls series brings out the desires and anxieties relating to femininity that are inherent in a patriarchal capitalist society and are internalized by women themselves.

In Yanagi's next series, My Grandmothers, on the other hand, the uncanny is evoked in a more liberating and life-enhancing way even though it depicts women approaching the end of their lives. The My Grandmothers series consists of photographic images of young women performing their self-images as old women. In order to create these images, the artist conducts a series of interviews with her models in which she asks them what they imagine they will be like fifty years from now. Interactions may last for as long as one year, involving the collaborative construction of a detailed chronology of imagined events leading to a particular moment in their future life; the model's future self as an old woman is gradually carved out of this story-sharing process. Yanagi then stages and photographs the scene. As a result, two stages of a woman's life are superimposed on one image in such a way that the images of both stages are revealed as imaginary constructs. These images, as I will demonstrate, both expose the compulsory aspect of gender and age performance *and* point toward the possibility of imagining and performing differently.

It is interesting that some of the images of future selves in My Grandmothers reveal how old fairy-tale formulas may inform the ways in which people understand and imagine their life stories as far as half a century into the future. In *Yuka* (figure 4.2), for example, an old woman with bright red hair roars across the Golden Gate Bridge in the sidecar of a Harley-Davidson driven by her boyfriend, who looks fifty years younger than she is.[2] This image seems to fulfill the standard fairy-tale wish that "someday my prince will come," apart from the fact that, here, "someday" is postponed until half a century later. This romantic interpretation is confirmed by the text written by the model and exhibited next to the photograph: "Indeed, I've had to turn down his marriage proposals, but he's obviously not giving up. . . . He says my big laugh brings good fortune" (*Miwa Yanagi* 55). That Yuka's dream has to be postponed so long raises a question as to the social and cultural constraints imposed on her as a young woman. In contrast to those portrayed in Elevator Girls, the women in the My Grandmothers series glow with vitality and individuality, as if old age is the golden age for women, when they can finally be freed from the social obligations expected of women of reproductive age. In their disguise of so-called second childhood, these women seem to regain access to their pre-Oedipal omnipotence. That Yuka's utopian vision of grandmotherhood is set in San Francisco, one of the places most often associated with the American Dream, also implies a criticism of contemporary Japanese society, which does not promise many options for women at any stage of their lives.

Twenty-eight-year-old Ayumi (figure 4.3), on the other hand, imagines herself becoming a Sleeping Beauty—in this case, not the heroine

FIGURE 4.2. Yanagi Miwa, *Yuka*, 2000. Chromogenic print, 1,600 x 1,600 mm. © Miwa Yanagi. Courtesy of the artist.

FIGURE 4.3. Yanagi Miwa, *Ayumi*, 2001. Chromogenic print, 583 x 1,000 mm. © Miwa Yanagi. Courtesy of the artist.

of Charles Perrault's tale but that of Kawabata's novella "House of the Sleeping Beauties." Ayumi's self-image as an eighty-year-old Sleeping Beauty, who sells not her body but her dreams to her male customers and never wakes up, can be seen as the uncanny double of those impassive young women in the Elevator Girls series; in the accompanying text, one of her customers says after spending a night with her: "Thanks to being shown such a wonderful dream, my body and mind have become completely relaxed" (*Miwa Yanagi* 44). *Ayumi* ironically rewrites both Perrault's and Kawabata's stories not only by turning the heroine into an old woman but also by giving her the ability to share her dream with others. The bright red bed linen seems to symbolize not the blood of menarche or defloration, sometimes considered to be the cause of the heroine's deathlike sleep in Perrault's tale, but the inexhaustible vitality of her imagination.

Although the accompanying texts indicate that the grandmothers imagined by Yuka and Ayumi both have grandchildren (*Ayumi*'s text is supposed to be narrated by her granddaughter), Yanagi claims that the expression *grandmothers* is not meant to exclude women with no grandchildren. It seems that she calls this series "grandmothers" rather than "old women" in order to emphasize not only familial but more broadly intergenerational bonding between women. In this context, "grandmothers" in the plural form refers to more than the two biological grandmothers we

FIGURE 4.4. Yanagi Miwa, *Ryuen*, 2002. Chromogenic print, 765 x 900 mm. © Miwa Yanagi. Courtesy of the artist.

all have; women become grandmothers to younger generations of women who will follow their paths. That the series has included three male models so far—*Eriko* (2001), *Estelle* (2003), and *Ryuen* (2002)—also shows that Yanagi's notion of grandmotherhood is not limited to its biological sense.[3] The model of *Ryuen* (figure 4.4), for example, is a young man posing as an old Buddhist nun. Ryuen mourns his deceased beloved in a doubly refracted form of cross-identification with her.

Yanagi's vision of her own future self offers another alternative to the notion of grandmotherhood conventionally confined to biological family relationships. In *Miwa* (2001) (figure 4.5), the artist herself is leading a group of children in a snowy wilderness. Her long blond hair and her black outfit closely resemble those of Maetel, the mysterious female character who guides the hero through his doomed journey in Matsumoto Leiji's popular manga and anime series *Ginga tetsudō 999* (1977–87; Galaxy Express),[4] which indicates that this image can be seen as the artist's ironic parody of, as well as her childhood admiration for, this cultural icon of female otherness. The text explains that Miwa, like Maetel, gathers children from all over the world, who become her "new offspring" (*Miwa Yanagi* 37). The feminist sociologist Ueno Chizuko associates this image with "The Children of Hamelin" and regards *Miwa* as reflecting the growing reluctance to have children among women who became adults during the economic recession in the 1990s and who are now "faced with a future devoid of hope" (64–65). However, it is also possible to interpret this self-portrait of the artist as an old female pied piper as leading her multiethnic band of stepgrandchildren to a world beyond a society that openly criticizes women who do not procreate, as is the case in today's Japan, a country suffering from one of the world's lowest fertility rates.

As the young women in the Elevator Girls series can be seen as the artist's alter egos, the old women in the My Grandmothers series reflect her own wishes for the future. Yanagi states in an interview that she did not include all the models who volunteered for her My Grandmothers project ("Miwa Yanagi"). Importantly, she turned down the images of

FIGURE 4.5. Yanagi Miwa, *Miwa*, 2001. Chromogenic print, 1,000 x 1,200 mm. © Miwa Yanagi. Courtesy of the artist.

grandmotherhood confined within the norms of the patriarchal family system, such as a grandmother living comfortably in a large house with her husband, her married son or daughter, and her grandchildren. As a result, male figures embodying patriarchal power are totally absent in the series.

In her video installation *Granddaughters* (2004), Yanagi reverses the temporal direction of My Grandmothers, going back more than half a century into the past. In *Granddaughters,* "real" old women talk about their childhood memories of their grandmothers. While remembering and talking about their grandmothers, they tend to slip in and out of an identification with the young girls they once were as well as with their grandmothers, whose age they have now reached. As is often the case with distant memories, their memories of grandmothers consist of both remembered and imagined events, and it is sometimes difficult to tell whether they are talking about their grandmothers or about themselves. For the viewer, the confusion is further heightened by the fact that the speakers' voices are dubbed with those of girls of their granddaughters' age. Yanagi's exploration of women's intergenerational cross-identification in her *Granddaughters* series draws even more heavily than in her previous works on the idea of telling and sharing stories among women across different generations, a theme that Yanagi pursues further in her next series dealing with traditional fairy tales.

RESTAGING GRANDMOTHER'S STORIES

Yanagi's *Fairy Tale: Strange Stories of Women Young and Old* (2007) is a book consisting of a series of photographic works based on traditional and recently created fairy tales. As its subtitle makes clear, *Fairy Tale* focuses on the relationship between young and old women represented in fairy tales. By foregrounding the periods before and after sexual reproductivity, Yanagi reappropriates the fairy tale in order to create a narrative space where women can break free from their socially prescribed roles and enact their fantasies protected from the demands of heteronormativity.

Fairy Tale opens and closes with a framing story in which a young girl recalls the stories told to her by her grandmother, who, in turn, claims to have heard them from *Suna onna* (Sand Woman; figure 4.6) when she was a little girl. Sand Woman is depicted as a hybrid figure with a young girl's legs and an old woman's hands, who tells stories while traveling in the desert. Her legs, parts of which are reflected in the pool of water below to the right, recall the webbed feet of the queen of Sheba, who bares her legs to cross a stream of water, which turns out to be made of a mirror.[5] In *From the Beast to the Blonde: On Fairy Tales and Their Tellers* (1994), Marina Warner discusses the significance of the theme of feet in the storytelling tradition, claiming that feet constitute "a recurrent sign of contrariness, and, in women, of deviancy" (121). In the case of Yanagi's Sand Woman, it is the disjunction between the immaturity of her legs and the synthetically emphasized gauntness of her hands, peeping from below and between her curtainlike cloak, that marks her monstrosity as a female storyteller. In Yanagi's Fairy Tale series, such discordant limbs figure as fetishized objects in the Freudian sense, as a metonymy for the mother's genitals. This uncanny female figure evokes not only Hoffmann's Sandman and Freud's interpretation of Hoffman's use of this bogeyman in northern European folklore, but also the women associated with sand in Abe Kōbō's novel *Suna no onna* (1962; *The Woman in the Dunes*) and in Gabriel García Márquez's short story "The Incredible and Sad Tale of Innocent Eréndira and Her Heartless Grandmother" (1972).[6] Whereas Freud sees the castration complex—Nathaniel believes that the Sandman tears out children's eyes, which Freud equates with the penis—as the basis of the uncanny effect of Hoffmann's story, Yanagi's fairy-tale images evoke the uncanny not through the castration threat in the Oedipal conflict between father and son but through women's imaginary relationship with the mother, especially a fantasy about the return to and subsequent ejection from the womb. For Freud, the womb, which he calls "man's old home, the place where once everyone lived ("The Uncanny" 151), represents the uncanny place par excellence as it subverts the familiar borderline between life and death; it is a place in the living body where death lurks as the repressed other of life, what should not and cannot be represented.[7] This equation woman-womb-death figures as the narrative space that represents not only an obstacle to be conquered, as in the case of the Sphinx, another female figure lurking in the desert, but also the home to return to at the end of the hero's journey, like the third daughter chosen by the hero in myth, folklore, and literature, as Freud discusses in his "The Theme of the Three Caskets" (1913). Yanagi's reworking of the images of women in fairy tales subverts the masculine desire for this topos, which immobilizes and marginalizes women in fairy-tale narratives.

FIGURE 4.6. Yanagi Miwa, *Untitled 1*, 2004. Gelatin silver print, 1,400 x 1,000 mm. © Miwa Yanagi. Courtesy of the artist.

Unlike her earlier brightly colored works, the Fairy Tale series uses black-and-white photography, which enhances the dreamlike, subconscious quality of the images. It also serves to foreground the indefinable nature of each character; the old witches' supposedly malevolent smiles may look rather innocent, and the young girls often appear more knowing than traditional stories tell us. This uncanny ambiguity is further intensified by the fact that all the models in Fairy Tale are girls aged between five and ten. Playing the parts of old women, the girls wear masks with exaggerated wrinkles and the hooked nose typical of a fairy-tale witch, but their bodies are undisguised, with lacy chemises revealing the smooth, plump limbs of young girls. Instead of trying to make the disguise look natural, Yanagi deliberately emphasizes the disjunction between the mask of a withered

FIGURE 4.7. Yanagi Miwa, *Mud Mask*, 2005. Gelatin silver print, 600 x 600 mm. © Miwa Yanagi. Courtesy of the artist.

crone and its wearer's girlish body. Yanagi also defamiliarizes traditional European fairy tales by presenting models of different races together in the same picture set against a Western-style background. The uncanny yet often humorous hybridity of these images destabilizes our naturalized notions of youth and old age, which are presented here as arbitrary and reversible; the models can exchange their roles by simply putting on or taking off their masks. An invented fairy tale titled "Mud Mask" (figure 4.7), in which a girl carves out an old woman's face on her sister's mud-covered face, makes a self-reflexive comment on this role-playing aspect. Reversibility and ambiguity are the underlying themes throughout Fairy Tale; they serve to dissolve the patriarchal value system that sets one woman to compete against another in terms of age, desirability, and knowledge.

Framed by the story of Sand Woman are scenes drawn from well-known, mostly European, fairy tales, each accompanied by a short text. Fairy tales, especially those written by such canonical writers as Perrault, the Grimms, and Andersen, are replete with binary oppositions typified by the female rivalry between the "angel-woman," who is good, beautiful, and young, and the "monster-woman," who is evil, ugly, and old (Gilbert and Gubar 36). Yanagi's Fairy Tale foregrounds the constructed nature of these oppositional images by restaging them as elements in coded role-playing that can be exchanged and transformed.

Yanagi states that the first work she made in the Fairy Tale series is based on Márquez's "The Incredible and Sad Tale of Innocent Eréndira and Her Heartless Grandmother," in which a beautiful fourteen-year-old girl and her grandmother travel together in the desert ("A Supremely Comfortable Place to Be" 220). The reversibility of the power relation between the young and the old is shown most schematically in the two works based on the story of Eréndira placed in the middle of Fairy Tale. Erendira I (figure 4.8) depicts the grandmother in control of her granddaughter's life, commanding impossible tasks like the wicked queen in fairy tales, whereas Erendira II (figure 4.9) shows the girl attempting to poison her grandmother by forcing her to eat the cake in which she and her lover secretly put "enough arsenic to exterminate a whole generation of rats" (Márquez 53).[8] These two opposite and opposing women, however, are closely tied to each other and eventually merge into one another. The Fairy Tale series is structured upon this ambivalent intergenerational female bonding, at once antagonistic and intimate.

FIGURE 4.8. Yanagi Miwa, *Erendira I*, 2004. Gelatin silver print, 1,000 x 1,000 mm. © Miwa Yanagi. Courtesy of the artist.

In Yanagi's recasting of fairy tales, the alleged opposition between young and old women is revealed to be deceptive. In her version of "Snow White" (figure 4.10), for example, the young girl and the old woman are shown as the mirror image of each other. The figure with her back to the camera appears to be the young Snow White, and the figure confronting the girl looks like her wicked stepmother. A closer look, however, will reveal that the masked figure is the reflection of the girl in the mirror. In the Grimms' "Snow White," it is the wicked stepmother who sees not her own but her stepdaughter's face in the magic mirror. She then sets out to kill Snow White, whose youthful beauty has defeated her in a beauty contest, which defines aging as a demeaning and fatal process for women. As Marcia K. Lieberman points out in "Some Day My Prince

FIGURE 4.9. Yanagi Miwa, *Erendira II*, 2004. Gelatin silver print, 1,000 x 1,000 mm. © Miwa Yanagi. Courtesy of the artist.

Will Come: Female Acculturation through the Fairy Tale" (1972), the "beauty contest" is "a constant and primary device" in many traditional fairy tales, a device she considers as a sign of patriarchal ideology (187). In Yanagi's version, however, the two stages of a woman's life are compressed into one figure in which the young self coexists with the old self, as they do in the My Grandmothers series. That the two women share the same destiny is indicated by the apple they are holding, which cannot be divided into two halves, one deadly and the other innocuous, as one side is only a mirror image of the other. This image offers an alternative reinterpretation of "Snow White" to the one given in the Elevator Girls series, in which women are preserved young and beautiful forever behind the glass shop windows.

FIGURE 4.10. Yanagi Miwa, *Snow White*, 2004. Gelatin silver print, 1,000 x 1,000 mm. © Miwa Yanagi. Courtesy of the artist.

Yanagi's recasting of "Frau Trude" (figure 4.11), the Grimms' moralistic tale about a girl thrown onto the fire as a punishment for her disobedience to her parents, captures the moment of the physical intimacy between the girl and the witch. The expected violence, foreshadowed by the bloodstained walls and curtains, is suspended by the two women's expressions, which are not necessarily suggestive of imminent atrocities. The faint smile on the old woman's face and the fascination on the girl's as she looks into the fireplace make their grappling look more playful and pleasurable than lethal. The accompanying text, "You will burn well if I put you on the fire" (*Fairy Tale* 50), can be interpreted as a playful threat exchanged between the women at a warm, intimate fireside. Yanagi's *Frau Trude,* therefore, brings the queer possibilities latent in this tale to the

FIGURE 4.11. Yanagi Miwa, *Frau Trude*, 2005. Gelatin silver print, 1,000 x 1,000 mm. © Miwa Yanagi. Courtesy of the artist.

fore, resonating with Kay Turner's lesbian interpretation of the tale: "Frau Trude's transformation [into the fiery devil] 'flames' the girl, ignites her, releasing her own transgressive lesbian desire. Moreover, by remaking the girl in her fiery likeness, the Frau recruits her as protégé" (263).

Yanagi's *Sleeping Beauty* (figure 4.12) also focuses on the intergenerational female bonding; the girl sits astride the old woman and holds the spindle which, in Perrault's story, puts the heroine to sleep. The power relation of the traditional tale is thus challenged in this recasting, with the girl threatening to put the old woman to sleep. At the same time, it is clear that the models can swap roles at any time by taking off or putting on the mask. The accompanying text reads: "'Time for bed.' 'I am not sleepy.' 'It is time to sleep.' 'Then you sleep first, Grandma'" (*Fairy Tale* 36).

FIGURE 4.12. Yanagi Miwa, *Sleeping Beauty*, 2004. Gelatin silver print, 1,000 x 1,000 mm. © Miwa Yanagi. Courtesy of the artist.

Yanagi turns Perrault's parable about female sexual passivity into a bedtime game played by two women in a spinning room with soft, cocoonlike balls of yarn rolling all over the floor, a womblike space pervaded with an aura of female-centered eroticism where the childlike flirting with death, which is symbolized by the spindle, serves to strengthen their homoerotic bonding; there is obviously no need for a prince to come and awake the girl to fully fledged sexuality. At the same time, this self-suffocating fantasy also seems to be suffused with a premonition of death, as suggested by the balls of yarn, which look as if they are stained with blood.

The aura of death also pervades Yanagi's *Little Red Riding Hood* (figure 4.13), which restages the rescue scene of the girl and her grandmother from the wolf's belly. The encounter between the girl and the wolf, a theme vital

FIGURE 4.13. Yanagi Miwa, *Little Red Riding Hood*, 2004. Gelatin silver print, 1,000 x 1,000 mm. © Miwa Yanagi. Courtesy of the artist.

to countless reworkings of this tale, is not the central focus here. The wolf is reduced to a flimsy zippered fur suit glistening with dark-colored liquid suggestive of blood. The huntsman, who rescues the two women from the wolf's belly in the Grimms' version, is completely omitted from the scene. It is not clear whether this is a happy ending or not; what is clear, however, is that the two generations of women have gone through a temporary death inside the wolf's body and have come back to life together, apparently without any male intervention. Yanagi's *Little Red Riding Hood*, like her *Snow White*, seems to celebrate the transformative potential arising from women's sharing of the same destiny. This focus on women's intergenerational bonding echoes Kiki Smith's lithograph *Born* (2002; figure 4.14), which also depicts the moment of the two women's bloody rebirths together from the wolf's belly. In Smith's

FIGURE 4.14. Kiki Smith, *Born*, 2002. Lithograph in 12 colors, 1,727 x 1,422 mm. Edition 28. Published by Universal Limited Art Editions. © Kiki Smith / Universal Limited Art Editions.

Born, both the girl and the grandmother are dressed in red cloaks that look as if they were made of blood gushing out of the wolf's belly and that also match the wolf's red tongue. The wolf's head and four limbs point upward as if to embrace the two female figures, whose arms are intertwined with each other's and whose feet are embedded in the wolf's belly. As I will discuss in the next chapter, the theme of women's affinity with the wolf is explored in Kōnoike's reworking of "Little Red Riding Hood."

Although Yanagi herself states that her Fairy Tale series has come to a close (Tani and Okamoto 24), the three new works recently added to her My Grandmothers series suggest that women's future self-images have come closer to the images of "old girls" in her Fairy Tale series, reflecting the change in women's self-perception after feminism began to make a deeper impact on Japanese society. In *Mitsue* (2009) (figure 4.15), for example, a considerably old woman—her neck is overemphatically skeletal—wearing a witchlike black hood and dress and holding sprouting bulbs in her hands, lies on the earth covered with moss and dead leaves. The accompanying text integrates her imminent death into the cyclic process of death and regeneration in nature:

> Listen to the breathing of the sleeping mountain,
>
> witnessing these blooms of frost.
>
> While some await spring, others pass away in winter.
> (*Miwa Yanagi* 12)

The subdued color tone of this image, cast in the dim sunlight of a cloudy winter day, resonates with the black-and-white world of the unconscious in her Fairy Tale series. That the artist actually grew the moss and the roses in her own garden over several months to realize the model's vision of the vegetation of a winter mountain indicates that the shared process of creation by the artist and the model has developed into a more organic one. Interestingly, *Mitsue* bears a striking thematic, compositional, and tonal resemblance to Kiki Smith's photograph *Sleeping Witch* (2000),[9] which also depicts a gray-haired woman—the artist herself, in this case— in a black hood and dress lying among fallen leaves with a black apple in her hand, suggesting that women across different cultures are imagining new stories about women in old age from the shared sources of traditional fairy tales in mutually resonant ways.

FIGURE 4.15. Yanagi Miwa, *Mitsue*, 2009. Chromogenic print, 1,300 x 1,300 mm. © Miwa Yanagi. Courtesy of the artist.

YAMAUBA, THE MOUNTAIN WITCH

Not all fairy tales that Yanagi restages are European; central to Yanagi's Fairy Tale is *A Lonely House* (figure 4.16), the only work drawn from Japanese folklore in this series. *A Lonely House* depicts the image of an old woman who at first appears very similar to the witch in European fairy tales but who actually is not completely assimilable to her European counterpart. Significantly, among all the female characters in Fairy Tale, she is the only figure who expresses deep compassion toward another woman.

"Hitotsuya" (A Lonely House), also known as "Ishi no makura densetsu" (The Legend of a Stone Pillow), is an oral legend associated with a place that used to be called Asaji-ga-hara (literally meaning "the field rank with short cogon grass") and is now a densely inhabited area of central Tokyo. As

FIGURE 4.16. Yanagi Miwa, *A Lonely House,* 2006. Gelatin silver print, 1,000 x 1,000 mm. © Miwa Yanagi. Courtesy of the artist.

cogon grass (a species of Asian tall grass traditionally used for thatching and fodder) is a topos symbolizing a desolate, uninhabited place in Japanese literature, the name of the place is associated with liminality, a space between human society and wilderness, reality and illusion, and life and death. The titular house that serves as a lodging for the night for the protagonist is also marked by liminality as a space to be passed through in transit.

The first written version of "A Lonely House" appeared in 1486 in *Kaikoku zakki* (A Memoir of Traveling around the World), a travelogue written by the Buddhist priest Dōkō, who claimed to have heard the story from a local old man. There exist several different versions of this story, most of which share the following basic plot. An aging woman and her beautiful daughter live in an isolated house in the middle of a desolate field. They regularly offer to give a night's lodging to travelers overtaken by nightfall. While the traveler is asleep, with his head on a stone pillow, the old woman kills him by dropping an enormous rock on his head and takes his money and other valuables. The two women make their living in this way until one day the daughter falls in love with one of the travelers and tries to save his life by taking his place in his bed. The mother realizes her mistake only after having dropped the rock on her own beloved daughter. In Dōkō's version, the daughter is forced to tempt men into their house just as Eréndira is forced by her grandmother to prostitute herself to make their living. In some variants, the old woman lives in the house by herself,[10] but as there are no variants without her, she seems to be the essential inhabitant of "A Lonely House."

The old woman in "A Lonely House" can be seen as a kind of yamauba. A yamauba often plays a similar role to the one played by a witch or a stepmother in Western fairy tales, but she is a more ambivalent figure than her Western counterparts.[11] She can be either beneficial or malevolent, humorous or cruel, nurturing or destructive. She is old, ugly, and wild, with her unkempt long white hair hanging down her shoulders and with her withered, bony chest and sagging breasts showing through her tattered clothes. She is a guardian spirit of a mountain and roves through the wilderness alone. The old woman in "A Lonely House" also lives at the outer edge of human society and embodies marginalized femininity in the Japanese folkloric imagination.

The story of the evil crone and her beautiful daughter living in a lonely house captured the popular imagination for its striking contrast between the two aspects of womanhood and was adapted for various literary, theatrical, and visual works. That it became an especially popular subject in *iki-ningyō* (realistic life-size doll) exhibitions, a public entertainment widespread in the latter half of the nineteenth century, indicates its visual as well as narrative appeal (Itō). Andō Hiroshige, a leading nineteenth-century *ukiyo-e* artist, visualized the scene in which the mother, whose white hair, deep wrinkles, and cadaverous features offer a sharp contrast with her daughter's beauty, peeps into the traveler's bedroom as her daughter prepares his bed (figure 4.17).

In many tales, a yamauba survives whether she succeeds in devouring a man or fails to catch him, leaving the possibility that she may be still

FIGURE 4.17. Andō Hiroshige, *Asaji-ga-hara hitotsuya ishi no makura no yurai* (The Origin of the Stone Pillow in a Lonely House in Asaji-ga-hara), 1843–47. The Digitized Contents of the National Diet Library.

roaming the mountains or awaiting unwary visitors in her lonely house. According to Kawai, this is due to the tendency in Japanese tales to leave open "the possibility of coexistence" with such potential destroyers as a yamauba or an ogre, who represent "the fearful quality of the unconscious" (*The Japanese Psyche* 44). Even when she dies, a yamauba tends to be either succeeded by her younger counterpart or given the posthumous power to yield benefits to human beings. In a folktale called "Ushikata to yamauba" (Ox-Driver and Yamauba), for example, a yamauba demands fish from a young man carrying a load of fish on his ox. After consuming all the fish, she demands the ox and devours it too. When she shows signs of wanting to eat the driver himself, he flees and comes upon a lonely house in the woods, which turns out to be the yamauba's dwelling. With the help of a young woman living in the house, he kills the yamauba, then marries the young woman.[12] This tale is similar to "A Lonely House" in its depiction of the cohabitation of two women possessing opposite qualities except that it ends with the death of the old woman rather than the young. We can, however, interpret the yamauba and the young woman as representing the two different aspects of one woman, that is, old and young, ugly and beautiful, and destructive and helpful. In some variants of "Ox-Driver and Yamauba," on the other hand, the yamauba's corpse turns into food, medicine, or gold, endowing the hero with wealth at the end of the story.[13]

A yamauba may devour everything, including human beings, but she may also help people, which makes her more complex than a typical villain in folktales such as an ogre or a wolf. For example, in "Ubakawa" (The Old Woman's Skin), a Japanese variant of "Donkey Skin" (ATU 510B), a beautiful girl who is abused by her stepmother leaves home and meets an old woman in the mountains who gives her a gown made of bark that transforms its wearer into an old woman. The girl in the guise of an old woman serves as a maid in a rich man's house until one day the rich man's son discovers her true appearance and marries her. In this tale, the yamauba is a beneficial figure, functioning as the donor in Propp's theory. A yamauba may also act as a facilitator of marriage in a more direct manner. In a tale called "Yamauba no nakōdo" (The Matchmaking Yamauba), the yamauba abducts a beautiful princess on her way to her wedding and delivers her to the house of a young man who is too poor to find a wife. The princess becomes fond of the poor man, and they live happily ever after, obtaining her parents' approval in the end. Although the yamauba in this tale at first forces the princess, she can be seen as the donor—not only for the young man, who does not have to make any effort to find an ideal partner, but also for the princess, who was about to marry a stranger chosen by her parents; it is as if the yamauba anticipated the young woman's unspoken wish to marry someone whom she likes however poor he may be.

Yanagi's images of young and old women in her Fairy Tale seem to be derived from the ambiguous nature of the yamauba and her equally ambiguous yet close relationship with the younger woman. In this respect, it is interesting to see the way episode fifteen in section twenty-seven of *Tales of Times Now Past* recounts a meeting between two women, a young lady-in-waiting who is pregnant yet unmarried and an old woman living alone in a dilapidated hut in the mountains. The young woman goes into the mountains in order to give birth secretly and abandon the child to its fate. The old woman sympathizes with the young woman's problem and offers shelter for her and her baby. Some time after the boy's birth, the mother discovers the old woman is a cannibalistic demon when she overhears the crone mutter, staring at the baby, "How yummy, just that one bite's worth" (Ury 63). The young woman flees with her son and, upon returning to the town, she has him adopted. She tells the story only when she herself becomes as old as the mountain crone. It remains uncertain what became of the latter.

In "In Pursuit of the *Yamamba*," Meera Viswanathan interprets the two women in this story as "a mirror, albeit distorted," of each other: "They represent the dialectic of female resistance, in which we see not so much an opposition between female characters as an internal struggle between production and consumption, between the sacrifice of self and the assertion of self, between order and anarchy" (245). Viswanathan's use of the metaphor of a mirror here brings us back to Yanagi's restaging of "Snow White," in which the young girl is facing the mirror image of herself as the old witch. Viswanathan also points out that, although most of the tales featuring a yamauba end in violence (protagonists either manage to escape the yamauba or are devoured by her), no actual violence appears in this story. Its absence may be related to the absence of an adult male character who, in other such tales, unwittingly disrupts the relationship between the two women. Nevertheless, it is notable that the boy child, however innocent and powerless he himself may be, again functions as intervention, opening up a rift between the two women, who were apparently living together harmoniously before his birth. This pattern also resembles "Snow White," in which the king, although largely absent from the story, tacitly invokes the patriarchal law through the mirror that frames two generations of women in an antagonistic relationship.

On the other hand, the fifteenth-century Noh play *Yamamba*,[14] usually attributed to Zeami Motokiyo (c. 1363–c. 1443), recounts an encounter between a yamamba and a young woman that involves no male interference. Hyakuma, a courtesan renowned for her dance performance representing the wanderings of the yamamba and thereby nicknamed Yamamba, seeks lodging in a lonely mountain hut on a pilgrimage to a temple with her entourage. The old woman who welcomes them reveals her identity as a real yamamba and asks Hyakuma to dance for her. When asked what a true yamamba is, the yamamba answers, "Whether demon or human, if it refers to a woman living in the mountains, it describes my situation" (Zeami 570), underscoring the possibility that any woman may become a yamamba when she leaves human society. She further blurs the boundary between herself and the young woman who impersonates her by quoting two Buddhist epigrams before she herself joins in the dance: *Zen'aku funi*—Good and evil are one—and *Shikisoku zekū, kū soku zeshiki*—Form itself is emptiness, emptiness itself is form.[15] The dissolution of polarities embodied by the folkloric yamauba figure is now cast in a Buddhist framework. The play aestheticizes the yamauba to such an extent as to disembody her, making her literally disappear into thin air like a mist at the end.

Given this history of the yamauba motif, what is most striking about Yanagi's recasting is that, instead of contrasting the images of the two opposite and opposing women, it depicts the old woman mourning the death of her daughter, a scene that has received but scant attention in visual representations of the tale. This image presents female antagonism in its most extreme form; the old woman has actually murdered the girl. The absence of the daughter, presumably flattened under the rock, suggests the merging of the two figures; the younger woman can be seen as an alter ego of the older woman, the part of her self that is beautiful and benevolent and capable of loving the other. On the one hand, the enormous stone seems to represent the old woman's hard, cold, and barren inside.[16] On the other hand, the loving manner in which she embraces the rock indicates the strong emotional bond between the two women, a connection that has long been cherished in a secluded all-female household. The sense of *aware* evoked in Yanagi's *A Lonely House,* therefore, can be seen as foregrounding the subversive potential of a yamauba as "a woman who loves a woman," like the witch-mentor in Anne Sexton's rewriting of "Rapunzel" (35).

DISMANTLING GRANDMOTHER'S HOUSE

Looking at the settings of the Fairy Tale series, we are reminded that so many of the canonized fairy tales are set in either an enclosed, domestic space or a complete wilderness, both separated from society. In fact, all the photographs in this series are set in one small room in the artist's own home-cum-studio. In an interview conducted in the same room used for the shooting of *Fairy Tale,* Yanagi explains the ambivalence she feels about Fairy Tale: "I feel a visceral connection to this kind of female expression, so while I appreciate that, at the same time I try to distance myself from it and look at my work objectively, arriving at a balance between the two. That very feminine part of me is the same thing as my wanting to be in this room all the time, it's a supremely comfortable place to be. It allows me to become very subjective, but it's also important that I am able to distance myself from it" ("A Supremely Comfortable Place to Be" 221). Yanagi's Fairy Tale certainly creates a narrative space where women can dissociate themselves from prescribed roles and act out alternative scenarios, but it is an uncanny utopia constantly undermining its own foundations, refusing to settle down with the formulaic happily-ever-after.[17] This "supremely comfortable place" will also be dismantled to reveal what lies backstage.

The motif of a fairy-tale house had already appeared in her previous series My Grandmothers. *Kahori* (2004) (figure 4.18) envisions the house in which she will be living fifty years on. Her face is not shown, but her gray hair and her bony hand show her old age. The most visible part of her body is her bare legs showing from beneath what looks like a frilly white Victorian nightdress for girls; interestingly, the legs look

FIGURE 4.18. Yanagi Miwa, *Kahori*, 2004. Chromogenic print, 640 x 800 mm. © Miwa Yanagi. Courtesy of the artist.

rather robust for her age and gender, destabilizing the stereotype of an old woman's frailty. The accompanying text reads:

> Ten years ago, I finally quit work and built my own house.
>
> Just as I dreamed, a little house deep in the forest.
>
> At present, not a single soul in the world knows me.
>
> I do not know if the world outside still exists.
>
> I do not know if I still exist. (*Miwa Yanagi* 22)

Her dream house, looking like a large Victorian house, however, is reduced to the size of a doll's house, indicating that she has far outgrown her girlhood fantasy. Kahori holds one side of the house as if she was reading a picture book and looks into this house within a house from outside, rather than being trapped inside the storyworld as an evil crone in Western fairy tales or a yamauba in "A Lonely House."

FIGURE 4.19. Yanagi Miwa, Sketches for *Lullaby*, 2010. Video installation, 12 min. © Miwa Yanagi. Courtesy of the artist.

In Yanagi's video installation *Lullaby* (2010; figure 4.19), the familiar and familial storytelling space of the fireside itself is defamiliarized and is dismantled to reveal its artifice. *Lullaby* features two women wearing prosthetic makeup, one playing the role of a girl and the other that of a grandmother, which suggests that this is another variation on her restaging of the relationship between women young and old. It is set in a Western-style living room with a fireplace where the grandmother sits on a rug with the girl's head on her knees, gently stroking her head and softly singing her a lullaby. The room, however, is visibly miniaturized to emphasize the disparity in size between the space and the bodies of the two women. The girl gradually reaches up her arms toward the old woman and suddenly springs up to force her to the floor. She then puts the grandmother's head on her knees and starts singing a lullaby to her until the grandmother turns the tables. The two women continue to engage in this vigorous battle over who will force down the other and sing her a lullaby.[18] The audience soon becomes aware that both women are in fact trained wrestlers as they start flinging each other down with a loud thud. The warm, cozy fireside, like the one drawn by the Victorian illustrator George Cruickshank for Edgar Taylor's translation of the Grimms' collection, gradually comes apart to reveal a wrestling ring on which the two women physically enact the power struggle. Then the camera pulls back to show that the ring is set on the rooftop of a skyscraper in the middle of a big city at night, with the streets below busy with traffic. *Lullaby* can be regarded as a twenty-first-century version of "A Lonely House"; the once desolate Asaji-ga-hara, as I mentioned, is now located right in the middle of the urban bustle.[19] Here, not only gender stereotypes in fairy tales but also the topos of the storytelling fireside symbolizing the traditional notion of home and family is dismantled from within, revealing its backstage reality. The two women, unperturbed by this epistemological dismantling, continue to grapple with each other, refusing to be contained in the roles and the space prescribed for women in traditional stories.

Yanagi's performative use of fairy-tale images exposes the culturally constructed nature of the representations of women and their lives that have become naturalized through the repetition of canonized fairy tales in various forms of cultural products. The doll-like beauty of young women in the glass coffin in the Elevator Girls series is undermined by the transgressive images of women in old age envisioned by the young women themselves in the My Grandmothers series. The young girls in the Fairy Tale series reenact the stories told by grandmothers so as to reverse, blend, and dissolve the binary opposition between the good, beautiful, young woman and the evil, ugly, old woman. In *Lullaby*, the familiar image of the grandmother telling stories by the fireside is also dismantled to reveal its nature as an ideological construct that relegates women and children to the socially marginalized sphere of home. Yanagi's juxtaposition of Japanese and Western narrative and visual traditions effectively produces a sense of cultural dissonance that allows viewers to defamiliarize the seemingly "natural" conventions of gender, age, race, and home in traditional fairy tales.

KŌNOIKE TOMOKO'S
WOLF GIRLS *in the* WOODS

Whereas Yanagi's restaging of fairy tales turns inward toward the intimate domestic storytelling space of the fireside, Kōnoike Tomoko's fairy-
tale art takes both the characters in fairy tales and the viewers of her
work out into the woods, another quintessential fairy-tale topos, where
magical encounters take place. In this chapter, I will read Kōnoike's visual
representations of the girl, the wolf, and the woods as reworkings of traditional stories about the heroine's encounter with a wild animal in the
woods, of which "Little Red Riding Hood" is probably the most famous.
Unlike Yanagi's self-reflexive juxtaposition of fairy-tale conventions from
Western and Japanese traditions, Kōnoike's works do not explicitly refer
to any specific fairy tales. As my analysis of Ogawa's novels in chapter 3 has shown, however, interpreting Kōnoike's visual images from the
perspective of feminist fairy-tale criticism will open up new possibilities
for reinterpreting and reimagining Little Red Riding Hood's encounter
with the wolf in the woods, a motif that has been reworked and reinterpreted by many feminist writers and critics in the West, beginning with
Angela Carter's seminal retellings in *The Bloody Chamber* and Jack Zipes's
groundbreaking collection *The Trials and Tribulations of Little Red Riding Hood* (1983). I will analyze the way in which Kōnoike's fairy-tale art
complicates the binary oppositions between human and animal, male and

female, and human society and nature underpinning many canonized fairy tales. I will also argue that her ongoing collective art projects combining art, oral storytelling, and handicrafts are an attempt to reconnect the storyworld to the actual lives of people who have been telling and retelling their individual and communal stories to each other, an artistic and social practice that reorganizes and revitalizes the dynamic relationship among stories, storytellers, and audiences.

ART, NARRATIVE, AND PLACE

The relationship among art, narrative, and place has been a central concern in Kōnoike's work from an early stage. Kōnoike was born in 1960 in Akita Prefecture in northeastern Japan. After receiving her B.A. in traditional Japanese painting from Tokyo University of the Arts in 1985, she worked as a toy and furniture designer for over ten years. She then returned to painting in 1997. Her first major solo exhibition, titled *Hiebieto kagayakashiku mezameru* (Awakening from the Cold Glitter), was held at Mizuma Art Gallery in Tokyo in 2000. Included in the exhibition were *Kekkan mori* (The Blood Vessel Woods), *Mori e iku? Soretomo ie e kaeru?* (Shall We Go to the Woods? Or Shall We Go Home?), and an early version of *Knifer Life* (2000–1), all of which contain the motifs of the woods, the wolf, and the girl. She has also explored these motifs in other forms; for example, she organized a series of workshops entitled Roppongi ni ōkami o hanate! (2007–8; Let Wolves Loose in Roppongi!), in which participants explored one of the largest commercial and entertainment districts in Tokyo, Roppongi (literally meaning "six trees"), with the aim of remapping the place by imagining themselves as wolves wandering in the woods. *Inter-traveller,* her largest solo exhibition, held at Tokyo Opera City Art Gallery in 2009, was later transported to the real woods of the Kirishima Open Air Museum in Kagoshima Prefecture in southwest Japan. In 2013, her first solo exhibition in the United States, titled *Earthshine,* was held at Gallery Wendi Norris in San Francisco. Although her works have been exhibited widely in both Asia and the West, she has worked mainly in Japan and for the Japanese audience.

Kōnoike's interest in narrative has led her to publish two picture books, *Mimio* (2001) and *Funsho: World of Wonder* (2011; Book Burning: World of Wonder), and to illustrate two Japanese novels based on old narratives of human-animal marriage, Shibusawa Tatsuhiko's *Kobiki* (1982;

The Story of the Enchanting Fox) and Sakuraba Kazuki's *Fuse: Gansaku Satomi hakkenden* (2010; Fuse: A Version of the Eight Dog Chronicle of the Satomi Clan). Shibusawa's story reworks Ōe no Masafusa's twelfth-century short narrative about a man enchanted by a fox into a dark erotic romance.[1] Sakuraba's novel is a metafictional rewriting of Takizawa Bakin's nineteenth-century epic novel based on the dog bridegroom story; it recounts the adventures of the hybrid offspring of a union between a woman and a dog, a creature whose ferocious nature becomes a threat to human society.

Kōnoike has also organized exhibitions combining visual images with folktales. At the exhibition held in her hometown Akita in 2011–12, titled *Tōhoku o hiraku shinwa ten, daiisshō* (Myths Opening up Northeastern Japan, Chapter One), she created an imaginary map of Akita by combining phrases from local folktales with installations by local artists and craftspeople. She first asked participants to make chance collages of fragments of local folktales in a manner reminiscent of surrealist collage poetry and then to create installations based on these randomly assembled folktale fragments. This collaborative remapping of northeastern Japan, a region that has been socially and culturally marginalized in modern times, invites the viewer to reflect on the interrelations among art, folktales, and topography. This project has led to her two other art and storytelling projects in progress in Akita, *Lodge the Art Museum Project* (2012–) and *Monogataru tēbururannā* (2014–; Storytelling Table Runners), which I will discuss later.

WOMEN AND ART

One of the most distinctive characteristics of Kōnoike's work is its sense-provoking texture. The creation of this texture begins with the laborious preparation of the canvas. In the case of *Knifer Life*, for example, the artist first coated the canvas with white acrylic, smoothed it with sandpaper, and coated it with acrylic again. She repeated this process as many as twenty times, using increasingly finer grades of sandpaper, until the surface was smooth enough for pencil drawing. This preparation, which took over three months, was followed by nine months of drawing fine lines in pencil and charcoal, and the whole process was repeated to add another scene on the left, which doubled the size to 180 x 810 centimeters.

Considering that this is a process involving almost endless repetition, one may wonder why the drawing has to be done with the hands, rather than with a computer, and what may be the effect of such an assiduous process.

Examined closely, the enormous number of fine lines on the canvas resemble less computer graphics than embroidery. In an interview with the psychoanalyst and critic Saitō Tamaki, Kōnoike compares the act of drawing to that of making stitches: "While I'm working, I feel less like I'm painting, but more like I'm sewing many lines onto paper." This comparison seems especially apt when we actually face the original canvas, whose texture foregrounds the physicality involved in the process of its creation. Asked about "femininity" in her work by Saitō, she replies: "Do you find femininity in my paintings? But the femininity you are talking about may come from the kind of concrete persistence required for painstaking embroidery" ("Intabyū" 25). It is significant that she locates the femininity in her work not in the motifs or themes represented but in the physical process of creating art, which she compares to the act of making a handicraft. Her emphasis on the "concrete persistence" involved in the creative process explains one reason why her work draws attention to the texture of its painterly surface which, for her, is an inscription of the movement and the rhythm of the hands "sewing many lines onto paper."

Kōnoike is not alone in reappropriating handicrafts as a female-oriented art form. Handicraft, as the element "hand" indicates, is closely associated with the body and the everyday life of the creator. Due largely to its traditional association with femininity, physicality, and domesticity, textile arts such as needlework and weaving have been marginalized within the institution of art, which places priority on fine arts as a more culturally valuable genre. Judy Chicago famously reappropriated stereotypically female arts such as sewing, embroidery, and weaving for her feminist revisioning of the role of women in culture and history in her collaborative installation *The Dinner Party* (1974–79), creating thirty-nine place settings for important women in myths and history. Chicago's work has inspired many women artists to revise stories and histories from a female-centered perspective. Kiki Smith has also used domestic skills and objects traditionally regarded as feminine and therefore marginal such as needlework, dolls, and home decorating. Kōnoike, although not explicitly describing her work as "feminist," has recourse to the metaphor of embroidery in order to foreground the physical and temporal dimensions of artistic creation hitherto underrepresented. She explains that the title *Knifer Life* is the name that she gave to the period of her life spent in drawing thousands of sharp lines with a pencil,[2] which also reveals her emphasis on the process rather than on the product.

The rhythmic physical repetition involved in the process of making handicrafts is intimately related to the craft of storytelling, as Walter Benjamin observes in "The Storyteller: Reflections on the Works of Nikolai Leskov" (1936):

> For storytelling is always the art of repeating stories, and this art is lost when the stories are no longer retained. It is lost because there is no more weaving and spinning to go on while they are being listened to. The more self-forgetful the listener is, the more deeply is what he listens to impressed upon his memory. When the rhythm of work has seized him, he listens to the tales in such a way that the gift of retelling them comes to him all by itself. This, then, is the nature of the web in which the gift of storytelling is cradled. (91)

According to Benjamin, the value of the craft of storytelling resides in its ability to make the listeners integrate or "sink" the story into their own experience by speaking to the deeper level of their mind. These contemporary women artists' uses of domestic skills and objects can be seen as a recuperation of more integrating forms of the communicative experiences that have been traditionally cradled in the intimate space of weaving, spinning, and storytelling.

Kōnoike's *Storytelling Table Runners* project (figure 5.1), in which local women patchwork and embroider patterns on table runners based on stories—individual and communal life stories of the past and the present—collected from the inhabitants of a small close-knit community in Akita called Ani, can be seen as a personalized and localized variation on Chicago's *The Dinner Party*. The activities of the *Storytelling Tale Runners* project includes holding tea parties in which local inhabitants gather around the table runners and talk about the images portrayed on them. Several gatherings have been held in Ani so far, and Kōnoike is planning to take this project to other countries in the future.

FIGURE 5.1. Kōnoike Tomoko, *Storytelling Table Runners*, 2014–.
Mixed media. Photograph by Hasegawa Takurō. © Tomoko Konoike.
Courtesy of the artist.

It is important to note that the specific locality of Ani is fundamental to Kōnoike's interactive and intermedial art projects based in this region. Ani had prospered in gold, silver, and copper mining since the fourteenth century until all the mines were closed down in the mid-twentieth century. Situated at the foot of Mount Moriyoshi, which spreads over about twenty square kilometers, it is also known as one of the largest bases of *matagi*, a group of professional bear hunters living and working according to their own specific beliefs and customs passed down from the past. Although it is now an underpopulated area, Ani has a unique history abounding in indigenous stories as well as stories brought in by miners coming from other regions and by bear hunters who used to travel throughout the country according to the hunting season. Recently, some people in Ani have been actively engaged in developing their own brand of cultural tourism and ecotourism on a voluntary and private basis, helping the community to be open to visitors from outside while strengthening bonds among its inhabitants. Kōnoike's *Storytelling Table Runners* project, which involves both female and male volunteers in Ani, has now become interwoven with these local movements.

GIRL MEETS WOLF

The image of a wolf-girl hybrid first appeared in Kōnoike's work in the part added to the earlier version of *Knifer Life* (figures 5.2 and 5.3), a painting that developed sideways like a narrative in a traditional picture scroll. When *Knifer Life* was first exhibited, it consisted only of the right half, depicting legs adorned with red trainers and white socks of the kind usually worn by a young girl, and the upper body completely covered with a swarm of numerous little daggers. A year later, another part was added on the left so that two figures, apparently the same girl, are placed side by side, as we see in figure 5.2. As the story unfolds, new characters are introduced; where the girl's upper body should be is now covered not only with daggers but also with several wolves looking as if they were sprouting from the girl's body. The extra pair of legs on the wolves' bodies seems to indicate their duality as the offspring of a human-wolf union. The move from the four feet of an animal to the two feet of human beings signifies the evolution from animality to humanity; the wolf girl's body seems to reverse this move and even transgresses a more radical species

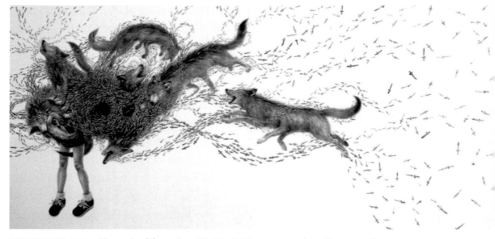

FIGURE 5.2. Kōnoike Tomoko, *Knifer Life,* 2000–1. Acrylic, pencil, canvas, and wood panel, 1,800 x 8,100 x 50 mm. Photograph by Miyajima Kei. © Tomoko Konoike. Courtesy of the artist.

boundary, retrogressing to the six legs of an insect. Moreover, the combination of the girl wearing red, the wolf, and the sharp instrument to cut open the wolf's belly recalls "Little Red Riding Hood" as its intertext.

Knifer Life also appears on the front cover of the 2004 reissue of Shibusawa's *The Story of the Enchanting Fox.* In Shibusawa's story, the girl born from a fox-human union seduces a prince just as a fox tricks men in the guise of a beautiful woman in Japanese folktales. As an animal adversary who tricks humans, the fox in Japanese tales can be regarded as an allomotif of the wolf in European tales with its gender reversed, the wolf being sexualized as a male seducer as in "Little Red Riding Hood." *Tales of Times Now Past,* for example, includes a story about a rich and lecherous merchant called Kaya no Yoshifuji who is bewitched by a fox impersonating a beautiful girl and is rescued by his family from a shabby storehouse that he was led to believe was a gentleman's house (Ury 102–5). Similarly, the nine-tailed fox, a mythical creature found in Chinese, Korean, and Japanese stories, transforms herself into a beautiful woman and seduces men in power. Kōnoike's visualization of the fox girl, however, is not eroticized in the conventional heterosexual—and often misogynistic—way. Unlike the overtly eroticized fox enchantress in Shibusawa's story, Kōnoike's representation of the human-animal

hybrid evokes the kind of eroticism that can be described as sensu-ous rather than sensual; the furry surface of the wolf's body and the dynamic rolling waves of tiny knives meticulously drawn by fine pencil lines make the viewer imagine a surge of clashing feelings—pleasures as well as fears—such as those that physical contact with a wild animal would provoke. Kōnoike's image of the fox enchantress at the end of Shibusawa's story (figure 5.4) seems to parody this male-oriented fan-tasy by reincarnating her as a pigtailed girl carrying a school rucksack on her back and wearing a miniskirt, knee-length socks, and trainers, the typical image of a schoolgirl fetishized in the Lolicon fantasy.

Kōnoike's Story Series, a series of paintings consisting of four chapters, takes the girl and the wolf into the woods. Story Series was made and shown in the reverse order, beginning with *Chapter Four* and moving backward toward *Chapter One*. When *Chapter One* was completed, all the four paint-ings in the series, measuring 220 x 630 centimeters each, were displayed on the four walls of a small exhibition room to form a circular narrative. In what follows, I will offer one possible reading of this series by relating it to "Little Red Riding Hood" and other stories about girls wearing red.

Chapter One (2006; figure 5.5) depicts wolves' tails growing out of a cluster of crystal blades on a glassy lake in a dark snowy forest. The

FIGURE 5.3. Kōnoike Tomoko, *Knifer Life* (detail), 2000–1. Acrylic, pencil, canvas, and wood panel, 1,800 x 8,100 x 50 mm. Photograph by Nakamichi Atsushi (Nacasa&Partners). © Tomoko Konoike. Courtesy of the artist.

FIGURE 5.4. Illustration for *Kobiki* (The Story of the Enchanting Fox), by
Kōnoike Tomoko. © Tomoko Konoike. *Kobiki*, by Shibusawa Tatsuhiko. Tokyo:
Heibonsha, 2004. 103. Courtesy of the artist.

FIGURE 5.5. Kōnoike Tomoko, *Chapter One*, 2006. Acrylic, sumi, Kumohada-mashi (Japanese paper), and wood panel, 2,200 x 6,300 x 50 mm. Photograph by Nakamichi Atsushi (Nacasa&Partners). © Tomoko Konoike. Courtesy of the artist.

parts of the crystal where the tails are breaking out are stained with what appears to be blood. If we interpret this image as a variation on Little Red Riding Hood's rebirth from the wolf's belly, the color red as a symbol of sexuality and violence in the traditional story is here replaced by the blood shed in giving birth to unknown creatures with wolves' tails. As in Smith's lithograph *Born* and Yanagi's recasting of "Little Red Riding Hood," the color red is reinterpreted as a symbol of regenerative power. In Kōnoike's Story Series, what stirs up the narrative imagination in the viewer is not the tension generated by the confrontation between the human and the wolf, which drives the traditional "Little Red Riding Hood" story; rather, it is the dynamics of the textural juxtaposition of contrasting feelings: soft, warm, furry, and organic on the one hand, and hard, cold, smooth, and inorganic on the other. *Chapter One* can be seen as a primal scene in which stories are constantly unfolding in the natural environment regardless of human intervention.

In *Chapter Two: Giant* (2005; figure 5.6), the gigantic figure of a wolf-girl hybrid in the form of a whirlwind of wolf fur flies across the blue sky over a vast green field. Crystal blades in *Chapter One* have been turned into colorful daggers flying around of their own accord, one of which is carried by a bee. That the wolf girl is wearing only one shoe suggests the story's connection with "Cinderella." (However, in later images she

FIGURE 5.6. Kōnoike Tomoko, *Chapter Two: Giant*, 2005. Acrylic, sumi, Kumohada-mashi (Japanese paper), and wood panel, 2,200 x 6,300 x 50 mm. Photograph by Nakamichi Atsushi (Nacasa&Partners). © Tomoko Konoike. Courtesy of the artist.

seems to have found her other shoe.) The red shoe in this image evokes the iconic ruby slippers in Victor Fleming's 1939 film *The Wizard of Oz*. Dorothy, caught in a tornado and swept into the magical land of Oz, goes through various adventures and finally acquires the magical red shoes that will take her home. The heroine of Neil Jordan's film *The Company of Wolves* (1984), based on Carter's story of the same title, also wears red shoes in the fairy-tale forest in the framed story, from which she eventually wakes up. In both films, the red shoes, which do not appear in the original stories, function as a cinematic token promising the heroine's eventual return home.

Chapter Three: Wreck (2005; figure 5.7) depicts multiple wolf girls flying around in a dark coniferous forest. This image of wolves among trees at night evokes the drawing by one of Freud's patients known as the Wolfman, so called after his childhood dream of a tree full of white wolves outside the bedroom window. In "From the History of an Infantile Neurosis" (1918), Freud interprets this dream as a symptom of the patient's castration complex caused by the trauma of witnessing his parents having "coitus a tergo"—that is, from behind like wolves—when he was a child (235). In Freud's interpretation of the Wolfman's dream, the wolf represents the castrating father, and the wolf's tail represents the penis. In Kōnoike's work, however, the dreamer *is* the wolf as the girl and

FIGURE 5.7. Kōnoike Tomoko, *Chapter Three: Wreck*, 2005. Acrylic, sumi, Kumohada-mashi (Japanese paper), and wood panel, 2,200 x 6,300 x 50 mm. Photograph by Nakamichi Atsushi (Nacasa&Partners). © Tomoko Konoike. Courtesy of the artist.

the wolf are merged into one body. Instead of evoking the fear of castration, Kōnoike's flying wolf girls seem to celebrate the duality and multiplicity of their existence. In "Wolf-Girl, Soul-Bird: The Mortal Art of Kiki Smith" (2005), Warner claims that Smith's *Daughter* (1999), a sculpture of a wolf-girl hybrid, "is the offspring of the wolf and Red Riding Hood's encounter in bed, the natural outcome of Angela Carter's fable 'The Company of Wolves,' which closes, 'See! sweet and sound she sleeps in granny's bed, between the paws of the tender wolf'" (52). Kōnoike's sleeping wolf girls in the woods can be also seen as another species born of the union between Little Red Riding Hood and the wolf.

It is also important that *Chapter Three* evokes other fairy-tale intertexts, especially through its use of the motif of red shoes recurrent in fairy tales, a motif that appears in this work as well as in *Chapter Two, Chapter Four,* and *Knifer Life.* In Andersen's "Red Shoes," for example, the heroine is punished for her vanity by being forced to dance all day and night wearing the cursed red shoes. She finally asks the executioner to cut off her legs, and her severed legs wearing red shoes keep on dancing, disappearing into the dark woods. The color red in Kōnoike's work, however, does not seem to be connected with the Christian notion of original sin inherent in women as in Andersen's punitive tale. *Chapter Three* can better be interpreted as an alternative sequel to Andersen's tale; deep in a dark forest, the girl's amputated legs in the red shoes meet the wolf, and they dance around together, weaving a different story from that of the upper half of the girl, who is said to have spent the rest of her life in repentance.

Neither do the red shoes in *Chapter Three* seem to indicate the cruel punishment at the end of the Grimms' "Snow White," in which the wicked queen is forced to wear red-hot iron shoes and dance herself to death. Rather, the wolf girls' red shoes seem to be more closely connected with the Grimms' lesser-known tale "Clever Gretel" (KHM 77), whose heroine "wore shoes with red heels, and when she went out in them, she whirled this way and that way and was as happy as a lark. 'You really are quite pretty!' she would say to herself" (*The Complete Fairy Tales* 350). In this story, the heroine is told by her master to cook two chickens for him and his guest. While preparing the chickens, however, she cannot curb her appetite and eats both of them herself. She then tricks her master into believing that it was his guest's doing and gets away with it. In "Whetting Her Appetite" (2012), Bacchilega argues that the red-heeled shoes in which Clever Gretel dances around happily signify her transgressive nature as "an artist of enjoyment," especially of autoerotic pleasure (32).

Furthermore, the closed eyes of the wolf girls also connect *Chapter Three* with the story of Sleeping Beauty, who sleeps in a castle surrounded by densely intertwined briars that defy human invasion. Kōnoike's wolf girls, however, do not seem to be waiting for a prince who will break the magic spell; rather, they invite the viewer to join in their exploration of the woods. The luxuriant trees with their gleaming leaves look like creatures with a will of their own, reaching out their cool, damp tentacles in all directions. The enormous heart in bright colors lying on the left-hand side may be seen as representing the heart of the forest itself as a living organism.

In *Chapter Four: The Return—Sirius Odyssey* (2004; figure 5.8), the final chapter of the Story Series, the wolf girl, now endowed with the translucent wings of an enormous insect, returns to the ocean, the home of all living organisms. As the title suggests, the terrestrial wolf seems to be finally united with its celestial counterpart Sirius, the star known as the heavenly wolf in Chinese astronomy. On the right-hand side hangs an insect that looks like a scarab beetle, regarded as a symbol of immortality in ancient Egypt, suggesting a never-ending cycle of rebirth and retrogression in Story Series, in which humans, animals, insects, plants,

FIGURE 5.8. Kōnoike Tomoko, *Chapter Four: The Return—Sirius Odyssey*, 2004. Acrylic, sumi, Kumohada-mashi (Japanese paper), and wood panel, 2,200 x 6,300 x 50 mm. Photograph by Kioku Keizō. © Tomoko Konoike. Courtesy of the artist.

and various other organic and inorganic elements of the woods all inter-mingle to weave their own stories.

In 2013, Kōnoike created the front-cover image for the new Japa-nese translation of Perrault's tales by the French literature specialist and feminist critic Kudō Yōko. *Ōkamizukin* (literally meaning "wolf hood"; figure 5.9) depicts a girl wearing a wolf's fur on which motifs from "Little Red Riding Hood" are portrayed. Her face, appearing between the wolf's teeth, is also partly covered with trees, suggesting the continuity among the girl, the wolf, and the woods. In this work, which explicitly refers to "Little Red Riding Hood," Kōnoike again emphasizes the girl's kinship with the wolf, rather than depicting the two characters as adversaries. Warner's reflection on the recurring hybrid animal figures in Kiki Smith's works also seems to apply to Kōnoike's wolf-girl hybrids: "[M]etamor-phosis enfolds values; it can punish, of course, by turning a barbarous king into a werewolf, or a boastful young woman into a spider; but the process also *transvalues* its subjects, so that a monster or a beast acquires another character, not by simply rising in a hierarchy, but by drawing new perceptions toward his or her condition. Smith's transformed beasts and monsters express her defiance, her subversion of accepted hierarchy in nature, of which female bodies are both a symbol and a part" ("Wolf-Girl,

FIGURE 5.9. Cover of *Ima yomu Perō "Mukashibanashi"* (Reading Perrault's *Contes du temps passé* Now), by Charles Perrault and translated by Kudō Yōko. Cover art by Kōnoike Tomoko. © Tomoko Konoike. Tokyo: Hatori Shoten, 2013. Courtesy of the artist and Hatori Shoten.

Soul-Bird" 52). As Yanagi's superimposition of the images of women young and old destabilizes the hierarchical notions of women's bodies and their lives, Kōnoike's merging of the girl and the wolf "transvalues" both figures, subverting the conventional perceptions of their nature and their place in a cultural hierarchy.

INTO THE REAL WOODS

In Kōnoike's Story Series, not only the girl and the wolf but also the woods go through metamorphosis; in her oeuvre, the woods do not figure as a mere backdrop for a human-centered drama. Her work invites us to read "Little Red Riding Hood" from an ecocritical perspective as a story calling for a reconsideration of our relationship with the natural environment. The injunction issued by Little Red Riding Hood's mother at the beginning of the Grimms' tale—"Do not stray from the path"—can be understood as a warning against the danger of leaving the human-made path demarcating human society from the wild forces of nature. Modern environmentalism, however, has pointed out the destructive consequences of anthropocentric exploitation of the woods, bringing to the fore the significance of what lies beyond paths cleared through the woods.

In this context, it is significant that "Little Red Riding Hood" inscribes both the danger *and* the attraction of the woods. In the Grimms' tale, the wolf lures Little Red Riding Hood away from the path into the woods as follows:

> Then he walked next to Little Red Cap, and after a while he said, "Little Red Cap, just look at the beautiful flowers that are growing all around you! Why don't you look around? I believe you haven't even noticed how lovely the birds are singing. You march along as if you were going straight to school, and yet it's so delightful out here in the woods!"
>
> Little Red Cap looked around and saw how the rays of the sun were dancing through the trees back and forth and how the woods were full of beautiful flowers. . . .
>
> So she ran off the path and plunged into the woods to look for flowers. And each time she plucked one, she thought she saw another even prettier flower and ran after it, going deeper and deeper into the forest. (*The Complete Fairy Tales* 126).

Urged by one of the natural inhabitants of the woods, which human beings also were once upon a time, the girl is awoken to the sensuous and sensorial pleasures provided by the flora and fauna of the untouched woods.

In *Gossip from the Forest: The Tangled Roots of Our Forests and Fairy-tales* (2012), Sara Maitland points out that "one of the central aspects of the northern European fairy story is that it takes place in the forest" and that "in fact, over half the stories (116 out of 210) in the 1857 edition [of the Grimms' collection] explicitly mention forests as the location of some part of the story, and at least another 26 have very clear forest themes or images" (16). Forests, for Maitland, evoke "a sense of enchantment and magic, which is at the same time fraught with fear" (10). It was in order to "challenge and examine" this fear that Maitland decided to walk alone into Glen Affric, an ancient pine forest in Scotland: "The forest was very beautiful, in a weird and ancient-feeling way. I discovered that, in reality, it was not 'fear' that I experienced, but something rather stranger. . . . [T]he forest gave me the same set of feelings and emotions that I get when I first encounter a true fairy story. For me, this is a visceral response and hard to articulate—a strange brew of excitement, recognition and peril, with more anticipation or even childlike glee than simple 'terror of the wild' because of the other sense that this is somewhere I know and have known all my life" (11).

Kōnoike's images of wolf girls in the woods similarly convey the visceral ambivalent response that Maitland associates with childlike feelings; in the far background of Kōnoike's *Chapter Three*, a roller coaster soars high up into the sky, calling up the simplest of those intense physical and psychological sensations accompanying temporary flight from the everyday experience of reality.

Kōnoike's picture book *Mimio* (figure 5.10) represents the next stage in her odyssey into the storyworld; in *Mimio*, the forest itself becomes the central character of the story. The narrative of *Mimio* follows the eponymous character who, like Little Red Riding Hood, goes through the forest alone and meets wolves and other inhabitants of the forest. All the illustrations in this picture book are black-and-white drawings except for the front cover, where vermilion is used for the title of the book, みみお, and for Mimio's fur, drawn in fine lines on a white background, paratextually evoking "Little Red Riding Hood."

Mimio is a soft, small, round, furry creature resembling a cuddly toy apart from the fact that Mimio has no face. Mimio is not an

FIGURE 5.10. Kōnoike Tomoko, *Mimio Original Drawings*, "Massuguni mukattekuru natsu, Takusan no kemono no fun no nioi ga suru" (The Headlong Rush of Summer, the Smell of Droppings from Countless Living Things), 2001. Pencil on paper, 397 x 544 mm. © Tomoko Konoike. Courtesy of the artist.

uncomplicatedly cute character with whom the viewer can easily make a narcissistic bond—the cuteness of characters such as Hello Kitty stems partly from the viewer's narcissistic identification with them as their innocent little selves[3]—but an ambivalent character defying any easy empathetic identification on the part of the viewer.

Having no mouth, Mimio is devoid of speech, but the story is mainly narrated from Mimio's perspective. Throughout the narrative, however, Mimio very rarely figures as a subject; instead, the narrative consists mostly of isolated noun phrases describing Mimio's perception of the surrounding natural objects and phenomena. Figure 5.10, for example, is accompanied by the following text: "The headlong rush of summer—the smell of droppings from countless living things" (22). Here, Mimio is supposed to be doing the smelling, but as Mimio obviously has no nose, the reader is induced to imagine the smell of these warm, freshly deposited droppings for Mimio. Mimio, whose name contains *mimi*, the Japanese word for "ear," plays a rather passive role for a protagonist, functioning mainly as a sensory receptor open equally to all the stimuli in its surroundings.

Mimio evokes "Little Red Riding Hood" not only through the commonality of the protagonist walking through the woods but, more strongly, through its sensuous and sensory representation of the woods, the natural environment that appears as a setting in many fairy tales, including "Little Red Riding Hood." In this recasting, Mimio's encounters with various elements in the woods such as flowers, trees, insects, earth, wind, fire, and water have the same narrative significance as encounters with wolves. Mimio's wandering in the woods again recalls the detour, quoted earlier, that the Grimms' Little Red Riding Hood takes in the woods.

Indeed, Mimio's story consists entirely of the sensuous detour for which Little Red Riding Hood is punished with death, albeit in a temporary form, in the Grimms' version. Through the sensuous textures of the natural elements perceived by Mimio, this picture book recasts "Little Red Riding Hood" as a story that is not centered on the confrontation between good and evil in man. Mimio is a creature constantly defined and redefined by what it feels with its own body; in other words, Mimio is embodied in its interaction with natural surroundings. The environment itself, therefore, is the main character of this story, with Mimio as a receptor responding to light, heat, smell, and other external stimuli in the forest.

Time in *Mimio* is circular in a more obvious way than in the case of the Story Series, beginning with the end of winter and going through spring, summer, autumn, and back to winter again at the end. When winter comes, Mimio's breath grows slower and fainter, and Mimio goes into hibernation, curling up on the snow: "Senses released into the darkness of the void. Their job complete—for now" (63). This ending brings the reader right back to the very beginning of the book, where senses are still asleep and where Mimio will soon begin to feel the light and the warmth of the sun and hear drops of melting snow again. Through Mimio's senses, the natural elements of the woods, which Little Red Riding Hood was told especially not to indulge in, begin to tell their own story.

When preparing for her exhibition at Kirishima Art Forest, Kōnoike was given an opportunity to enter the deepest part of the woods usually designated as a no-entry area, and this experience had a significant impact on her work. She later observed that, in her open-air installations, she tried to "convey to the viewer the bodily sensations and the textures that she felt while looking at the woods" (Sakamoto 35). The recurrent motif of flying knives in her work can be seen as a metaphor for the

FIGURE 5.11. Kōnoike Tomoko, *Wakusei wa shibaraku yuki ni ōwareru* (The Planet Is Covered by Silvery Sleep), 2006. Mixed media (mirror, wood, styrofoam, aluminium, etc.), 1300 x 2700 x 850 mm. © Tomoko Konoike. Courtesy of the artist.

intensity of the visceral feelings, fears as well as excitement, felt by the artist in the deep forest.

The knives become incorporated into the wolf girl's body in the installation *Wakusei wa shibaraku yuki ni ōwareru* (2006; The Planet Is Covered by Silvery Sleep; figure 5.11), a six-legged wolf whose surface is covered with mirror shards. A long, wide strip of wolf fur which the wolf trails—real fur taken from wolves killed to protect livestock in Mongolia—indicates that the wolf-girl hybrid has undergone another stage of metamorphosis. In this work, the girl is no longer visible, presumably having merged completely with the wolf, whose extra pair of legs is the only visible indication of its dual existence. The mirror fragments, which replace the knives in her earlier works, add another layer of symbolic meaning to her wolf girls. In myths and fairy tales, mirrors do not simply reflect appearances but refract the surfaces of reality to reveal another level of meaning hidden beneath them. The mirror fragments covering the wolf's body refract the images of reality, inviting viewers to look beyond the threshold of everyday reality.

FIGURE 5.12. Kōnoike Tomoko, *Kemono no kawa o kaburi, kusa no amimono* (Donning Animal Skins and Braiding Grass), 2011. Mixed media (mirror, wood, styrofoam, aluminium, etc.) 1170 x 3180 x 550 mm. © Tomoko Kōnoike. Courtesy of the artist.

When this wolf-girl figure is taken out of the art gallery into a real forest in the installation *Kemono no kawa o kaburi, kusa no amimono* (2011; Donning Animal Skins and Braiding Grass; figure 5.12), the mirror shards covering her body reflect the trees and the sky around her, blurring the boundary between the wolf girl and the woods. This work was temporarily installed in Chichibu, the mountainous region in Saitama Prefecture known as the place of the origin of wolf worship. The title of this installation suggests that inside the wolf there is a girl braiding grass, an act of making handiwork that has a transformative power, as in the Grimms' "The Six Swans" (KHM 451), in which the heroine weaves asters to make shirts that will break the spell.

It is interesting that Kōnoike's images of wolf girls in the woods find an echo in the Canadian poet Cornelia Hoogland's *Woods Wolf Girl* (2011), a collection of poems inspired by "Little Red Riding Hood" and set in the woods on the west coast of Canada. Although geographically distant, the two places depicted in their works are both green, snowy regions where wild animals live close to human habitats. One of the poems in *Woods Wolf Girl*, titled "Mother," describes the severe beauty of the forest and its lupine inhabitant:

The forest in point form.

Hundreds of trees

straight-up as knives; so many sprung

blades so

    sure of themselves.

    In the open field a wolf

    pats the grass, leaps up on all fours,

        lands.

Kills what she can. (18)

This image of trees as sharp and straight as knives and a female wolf leaping up on all fours to kill resonates with Kōnoike's visualization of wolf girls in the woods discussed in this chapter. The senses evoked by nature connect the two remote parts of the world, reminding us that stories such as "Little Red Riding Hood" arise where culture and nature intersect. It is at this intersection that transcultural connections can be made.

FIGURE 5.13. Kōnoike Tomoko, *Lodge the Art Museum Project*, 2012–. Mixed media. © Tomoko Konoike. Courtesy of the artist.

In her ongoing *Lodge the Art Museum Project* (figure 5.13), Kōnoike takes the viewer out into a mountain forest. The project consists of a series of installations exhibited in a mountain shelter, a wooden hut that sits on Mount Moriyoshi in Akita at about 1,275 meters above sea level. In order to see the installations, viewers first have to get to the foot of the mountain by train, air, or car (by whichever means, it takes more than five hours from Tokyo) and then climb the mountain (one can also take the gondola up to a certain point and then walk). When I first visited the site in early spring, the mountain was still covered in deep snow, so I had to borrow snowshoes from the mountain guides' office. I was traveling on my own, trying not to lose my way on a snowy mountain. When I arrived in the hut half buried in snow, there was nobody there except the wolf girl sitting on the edge of the boat high up above my head. Kōnoike's *Lodge the Art Museum Project* thus turns the audience into Little Red Riding Hood themselves, who would walk through the mountain forest to a little hut where real and imaginary creatures await them on the threshold of human society.

As we have seen, Kōnoike's work refracts the motif of the girl's encounter with the wolf in the woods using different media, contexts, and methods, from paintings and illustrations to collaborative art projects and public art installations. Her intermedial reimaginings of this motif, anchored to her own bodily sensations, allow us to reenter the storyworld of "Little Red Riding Hood" with new awareness and excitement and to connect with aspects of the world with which we have lost in touch or that we have yet to discover. Kōnoike's work transports the storyworld of Little Red Riding Hood into the real woods in an attempt to imagine and feel what lies beyond the anthropocentric understanding of the world. For Kōnoike, nature is intimately bound up with the social and cultural environment of which it is a part as well as being the suppressed Other; her *Storytelling Table Runners* project, in which she collaborates with those living at the foot of Mount Moriyoshi, is an attempt to give expression to voices that have been underrepresented in official histories and stories in Japan, and have never been translated into other languages. At the same time, her localized projects involving the people, the history, and the physical environment of a small traditional community also reveal transcultural themes found in fairy tales around the world, reaffirming the significance of the fairy tale as a rich repository of stories of interactions among human beings, animals, and nature; in her case, it is through specific locality that a shared experience emerges and gives voice to hitherto unheard stories. Such movements back and forth between the storyworld and the storytelling space reinvigorate both our individual lives and the fairy-tale tradition, remapping the genre's book-centered and Eurocentric canon.[4]

EPILOGUE

In closing, I return to the two guiding questions I posed in the introduction: "What kind of criticism would be needed to analyze fairy-tale adaptations produced in a non-Western culture? What insights would such an analysis in turn bring to current fairy-tale re-creations and research in the West?"

My close textual analyses of the four Japanese women's works demonstrated that a critical framework developed by Western feminist fairy-tale scholarship can illuminate Japanese texts without overdetermining their interpretations. At the same time, it also became clear that, in order to approach a non-Western text, we need to take into consideration the various kinds of literary and artistic conventions that the text brings into play. This requires a certain amount and level of immersion in a specific cultural environment necessary to gain enough knowledge of its historical, social, and linguistic contexts. A more precise transcultural remapping of the genre becomes possible through a process of collaborations and conversations between researchers with different cultural and linguistic backgrounds. By describing the reception, transformation, and study of fairy tales in Japan in the light of Euro-American feminist fairy-tale criticism, this book tried to bring to light the complex ways in which transculturalism and localism compete with as well as complement each other in a non-Western cultural context.

One important advantage of this kind of cross-cultural approach is that it challenges the universalization of Euro-American norms. It can serve to prevent Euro-American scholarship from falling into a trap of remarginalizing non-Western cultures by focusing on the aspects of those cultures that fit into preexisting stereotypes and therefore tend to be more readily available in English translation. In the case of Japanese texts, there have appeared several innovative studies in English on fairy-tale adaptations in Japanese manga and animation films.[1] On the one hand, such studies have expanded the scope of fairy-tale cultural and film studies in the West and, as I mentioned in chapter 1, Japanese girl studies can be an effective feminist approach to fairy-tale adaptations in various fields of contemporary popular culture, an area of research that this book does not cover but that needs to be pursued further. On the other hand, putting an emphasis on a certain aspect of Japanese culture can lead to the reinforcement of the old dichotomy between the irrational, feminine, and childish Orient and the rational, masculine, and mature West. Looking closely at women's creative fairy-tale adaptations for adult audiences, in my view, serves to demystify such typecasting of contemporary Japanese culture and to offer a more inclusive picture of that culture. For this purpose, I made a distinction between the reclaiming of "wonder" by the women writers and artists discussed in this book and the culture of kawaii, which is more popularly associated with contemporary Japanese culture in the West, and focused my analyses on the aspects of their works that resist and subvert the eroticization of girls in the Lolicon fantasy perpetuated by both men and women.

My antiessentialist approach, informed particularly by Euro-American post-structuralist feminist literary criticism, in turn, offers a new way of understanding critical and creative discourse on fairy tales in Japan. As I argued in chapter 1, the Jungian interpretation of fairy tales proposed by Kawai has been influential in the general understanding of the genre in Japan, which has led to the essentialist generalization of Japanese tales as feminine, ambiguous, and closer to nature, and of Western tales as masculine, logical, and human centered. My case studies of contemporary Japanese works from a cross-cultural and feminist perspective challenge Kawai's essentializing of the Japanese fairy tale as a reflection of the Japanese psyche and femininity conceived as the exact opposite of the Western psyche and masculinity. The four women's works do support Kawai's contention that the fairy tale is closely connected with the depth of the psyche but, more important, they offer more complex views of women and their relationship with the Other through their uses of fairy tales in both Western and Japanese traditions.

As I pointed out in chapter 1, Shibusawa's translation, criticism, and adaptation of European fairy tales contributed significantly to adult readers' recuperation of the genre while at the same time exoticizing European fairy tales as expressions of sexual and violent unconscious desires and remarginalizing women. Shibusawa exerted a formative influence on the late twentieth-century Grimm boom, a phenomenon that reflects the conflicting process of Japan's Westernization since the late nineteenth century and the social and sexual repression to which women have been subjected in a male-dominated society. The representations of women, violence, and sexuality in the four women's fairy-tale adaptations displace Shibusawa's othering of both the West and Woman in his critical and creative reworking of the fairy tale.

The works by the four women writers and artists represent varied involvements with the fairy tale across different cultures and media in today's Japan. Tawada's critical reworking of the animal bride and bridegroom tale parodies universalizing structuralist precepts and creates a liberatingly destructuring tale of never-ending metamorphosis. Her "The Bridegroom Was a Dog" illustrates the innovative potential of bringing the Western framework into dialogue with Asian variants to generate a new, dissonant model. Her intermingling of different fairy-tale traditions resists both Kawai's essentializing of differences and Shibusawa's eroticization of differences.

Ogawa's *Hotel Iris* takes Kawai's modified Jungian framework to its extreme and emerges from its constricting fantasy with new awareness. Ogawa's Bluebeard story disrupts the male-oriented Lolita paradigm of desire by revealing its stagnating logic of interdependence between the desiring, sadistic male and the desired, masochistic female. Its focus on the girl's inner conflict with and rebellion against her mother also counteracts Shibusawa's notion of the virginal girl as pure passivity. In Ogawa's reimagining, the bloody chamber comes to function paradoxically as a site of female creativity and authorship, as the heroine, the only survivor in Bluebeard's castle, starts recounting her exploration into the unknown realm of her body and mind.

Yanagi's reconfiguration of the fairy-tale images of women young and old destabilizes the hierarchical opposition between the good, beautiful, and young princess and the evil, ugly, and old witch underpinning canonical fairy tales in the West. The juxtaposition of different cultures and bodies in her fairy-tale photographs produces a sense of cultural dissonance that disrupts the assumed universality of Western fairy tales. This dissonance in turn opens up a space for imagining lives and stories of women that are different from the familiar models. Eroticism evoked in the scenes of intergenerational female bonding offers an alternative mode of female desire to those based on the Jungian-Kawaian and the Sadeian-Shibusawan paradigms.

Kōnoike's image of the wolf-girl hybrid de-eroticizes Shibusawa's fetishization of women as both pure virgins and devouring seductresses, which also underlies the Lolicon fantasy. At the same time, her reappropriation of animality for women does not collude with the Jungian-Kawaian equation of woman with nature; her works present the relationship between women and nature not as harmonious and fixed but as precarious and constantly unfolding, charged with imminent danger as well as a sense of wonder—just as one would feel walking alone in the woods like Little Red Riding Hood. Furthermore, her communal projects combining art and oral storytelling point to a new way of invigorating the interaction between the storyworld and the actual lives of people telling and retelling stories.

From the dog bridegroom to the wolf girl, this book showcases a wide range of women's uses of fairy-tale motifs and patterns in contemporary Japanese literature and art. By discussing them in the contexts of both Japanese and Euro-American fairy-tale criticism, I hope to weave another pattern into the fairy-tale web, making its design even more complex and intriguing—as it is becoming in this age of global interweaving of diverse cultures.

One of the limitations of this book's approach is that it does not concentrate on a particular motif or tale type; following a more specific pattern of the development and variations of a certain motif or plot will yield a deeper insight, furthering our understanding of the genre. The animal bride and bridegroom tale type, which has inspired many creative and critical responses both in Japan and abroad, is one important area of research that needs to be explored more systematically.[2] Another line of inquiry worth pursuing is the interactions among fairy-tale adaptations across media in contemporary Japan. At the moment, however, intermedial cross-fertilization in this area seems less noticeable in Japan than in the West, mainly due to the lack of interpretive discourses on contemporary fairy-tale adaptations. As has been the case in the West, interactive dialogues between critical and creative practices will be the key to the further development of feminist fairy-tale culture in Japan. In this respect, it is interesting that the writers and artists discussed in this book have been increasingly turning toward more interactive media, for example, Tawada's public readings and collaborative performances with artists, actors, and musicians, Ogawa's series of dialogues with scientists, Yanagi's theater productions, and Kōnoike's collective art projects. Fairy-tale critics in Japan also need to reciprocate this move by reaching beyond academic discourses to take part in the re-creation of fairy tales in other spheres.

What emerges as the specificity of the Japanese fairy-tale adaptations discussed in this book evidences the imbalance of power in global circulations of literature pointed out by Cécile Sakai, an idea mentioned in the introduction. Shared among the critics, writers, and artists discussed in this book is a sense of cultural dissonance and marginality in their encounter and negotiation with Western culture. In many areas of contemporary culture, including literature and art, western Europe and North America still remain the cultural norm while non-Western cultural products circulate globally as culturally marked, as something that needs to be either assimilated into the dominant form or exoticized as the cultural Other, a system of cultural processing that would deflect the audience's deeper appreciation of each work's unique potential. This book discussed two ways of counteracting this imbalance of power discernible in the reception of contemporary Japanese literary and artistic works: one way, represented by the works by Tawada and Yanagi, is to self-consciously foreground cultural dissonances so as to problematize the assumed universality of Western norms while the other approach, found in the works by Ogawa and Kōnoike, causes transcultural elements to emerge from localized concerns in such a way as to dissolve cultural hierarchy. These women writers' and artists' sense of cultural dissonance and marginality is also entwined with their concerns about the constricting notions of women and their lives that obtain in a still largely male-dominated Japanese society. Important insights will be afforded by comparing these Japanese texts with other contemporary fairy-tale adaptations in Western and non-Western cultures; those that immediately come to mind include the British novelist Helen Oyeyemi's *Mr Fox* (2011) and *Boy, Snow, Bird* (2014), the Australian novelist

Danielle Wood's *Mothers Grimm* (2014), the Korean artist Chan-Hyo Bae's Existing in Costume series, and the Canadian photographer Dina Goldstein's Fallen Princesses series (2009).

One way of making visible what Damrosch calls the incommensurability of different cultures is to make a map—or, more precisely, a web—of existing cultural products that can be connected thematically or morphologically with each other across cultural boundaries. By tracing the threads of the fairy-tale web with eyes that are both transcultural and culturally sensitive, we can begin to see how different cultural traditions intersect and clash with each other, making new connections and generating more intricate patterns of forms and meanings. The metaphor of a web is especially encouraging because, however complex the web may grow, it nevertheless remains a network, an arrangement of interconnected threads, with each new thread always connected with a preexisting one. Cultural identities and our own identities emerge through this process of connecting and reconnecting threads to make out new patterns in the ever-growing fairy-tale web.

NOTES

INTRODUCTION

1. Fairy-tale studies informed by Western theories and literary reworkings of folk and fairy tales also appeared in Japan during the 1970s. As I will argue in chapter 1, however, it was not until the 1990s that a truly dialogic relationship between criticism and retellings in the sense Joosen defines began to be observed.

2. Japanese names throughout this book are given in the Japanese order, with the family name first, except for those whose names are commonly known abroad in the Western order, such as Yoko Ono.

3. See, for example, Catherine Orenstein's analysis of Smith's sculpture *Daughter* (1999) in her study *Little Red Riding Hood Uncloaked* (170–72), Marina Warner's discussion of Smith's wolf-girl figures in "Wolf-Girl, Soul-Bird," and Sarah Bonner's analysis of the visual development of "Little Red Riding Hood" in the works of Smith, Paula Rego, and Gérard Rancinan in "Visualising Little Red Riding Hood."

4. For example, Smith's *Born* appears on the front covers of the fairy-tale journal *Fairy Tale Review,* edited by Kate Bernheimer; Cornelia Hoogland's book of poetry *Woods Wolf Girl,* which the poet states was inspired by Smith's work; and Jack Zipes's critical work *The Irresistible Fairy Tale.*

5. For example, the Australian artist and art historian Jazmina Cininas's The Girlie Werewolf Project (2002–) creates linocut portraits of influential women as "girlie werewolves," including portraits of Kiki Smith, Angela Carter, Cristina Ricci, and the heroine of the Japanese animation film *Mononoke-hime* (dir. Miyazaki Hayao, 1997; Princess Mononoke).

6. All quotations from works cited only in Japanese in the works cited list are given in my own translation.

CHAPTER 1

1. According to Kim Jong Bom, *Konjaku monogatarishū* contains twenty-eight tales relating to Korea even though there is no separate section devoted to Korean tales.

2. The origins of "Urashima Tarō" date back to *Nihon shoki* (c. 720; The Chronicles of Japan).

3. In *Nihon no kindaika to Gurimu dōwa: Jidai ni yoru henka o yomitoku* (Japan's Modernization and the Grimms' Tales: Interpreting the Changes over Time), Nagura states that the five key ideas that composed Herbart's concept of individual maturation—Inner Freedom, Perfection, Benevolence, Justice, and Equity or Recompense—can be mapped onto the five main virtues of Confucianism: Humanity, Righteousness, Propriety, Knowledge, and Integrity, to be made suitable for nationalistic moral education (12).

4. The tale's earlier forms and its use as war propaganda are discussed in Antoni.

5. For a detailed discussion of the historical context of the Momotaro paradigm, see Dower 252–59.

6. For a survey of the reception of the *Arabian Nights* in modern Japan, see Sugita.

7. The 1960s also saw the emergence of creative theatrical adaptations of Western fairy tales. As Steven C. Ridgely shows, Terayama Shūji's (1935–83) series of dramatic reworkings of "Bluebeard" began with his 1961 radio play *Aohige to ichigo-jamu* (Bluebeard and Strawberry Jam). Betsuyaku Minoru's (1937–) *Macchiuri no shōjo* (*The Little Match Girl*) was performed to a wide critical acclaim in 1966. Betsuyaku's play tells the story of a woman who, as a little girl, used to sell matches to men and light the inside of her skirt for them.

8. It is notable that the translator, writer, and poet Yagawa Sumiko (1930–2002), who was Shibusawa's first wife, published the translation of Mary De Morgan's collection of literary fairy tales *The Windfairies* (1900) in 1979, introducing Victorian fairy tales by a then virtually unknown woman writer into the publisher Iwanami's influential children's literature series.

9. The pronunciation *yamauba* is usually used to refer to the mythical and folkloric figure, whereas the nasalized form *yamamba* is applied to the literary representations of the figure that first appeared in the fifteenth century. This book will use the form *yamauba* to underline the folkloric origin of the figure except when discussing literary texts that use the form *yamamba*.

10. *Yamambatachi no monogatari: Josei no genkei to katarinaoshi* (The Stories of Mountain Witches: Female Archetypes and Their Retellings), edited by Mizuta Noriko and Kitada Sachie, celebrates the transgressive potential of a yamauba represented in literary, historical, and artistic works in Japan. See also Michiko N. Wilson's discussion of Ōba's reworking of yamauba tales.

11. In the epilogue of her book, Noguchi expresses her fury at the total disregard her early works met and states that she decided to reproduce her 1977 article on Rölleke unrevised in order to "settle an old score" (192).

12. The link between Kurahashi's *Otona no tame no zankoku dōwa* and Carter's *The Bloody Chamber* was first made in Fujikawa Yoshiyuki's afterword in the translation of *The Bloody Chamber* in 1992; since then, this comparison has become widely accepted by Japanese critics. See, for example, Kotani Mari's afterword to the paperback edition of the translation of *The Bloody Chamber* in 1999, Ikoma Natsumi's *Yokubō suru bungaku,* and Murai's "The Translation and Reception of Angela Carter's Work in Japan."

13. The Ghibli film *The Tale of the Princess Kaguya* also uses this motif from "The Lady Who Loved Insects" in its characterization of the heroine who first refuses to conform to the role assigned to women.

14. In "The Queen's Looking Glass: Female Creativity, Male Images of Women, and the Metaphor of Literary Paternity," the opening chapter of *The Mad Woman in the Attic*, Gilbert and Gubar see the antagonism between the wicked queen and Snow White as a paradigmatic instance of male-generated twin images of "the monster-woman and the angel-woman" (36). They further argue that the mirror, which represents the voice of the king internalized in the queen's mind, sets the two women against each other.

15. The affinity between Kurahashi and Shibusawa is also evident from the fact that one of Kurahashi's short stories is included in Shibusawa's anthology of erotic and/or cruel stories titled *Ankoku no meruhen* (1971; Dark Märchen).

16. In 2010, two Chinese publishers, apparently believing that they had found the "real" versions of the Grimms' tales, published the translation of Kiryū's collection, which ended up in the children's book section by mistake.

17. In 1999, Mastumoto in fact sued Kiryū and their publisher for plagiarizing over a hundred lines from her story collection. They reached a compromise in court whereby Kiryū agreed to rewrite the parts in question. Kiryū also admitted plagiarizing from Suzuki's introductory book. For details, see Ikeda and Maruyama.

18. Sandra Buckley's *Broken Silence: Voices of Japanese Feminism* (1997) gives an overview of feminism in Japan up to the 1990s, including an interview with the leading feminist sociologist Ueno Chizuko.

CHAPTER 2

1. By "world literature," I mean newly emerging works that not only participate in but also reflect on the processes of literary globalization. Doug Slaymaker's *Yōko Tawada: Voices from Everywhere* places Tawada's work in the context of this redeployed notion of world literature.

2. The extracts from "The Man with Two Mouths" appear in English in Margaret Mitsutani's "Tawada Yōko's 'The Man with Two Mouths.'"

3. In one episode, Till thwarts a knight's attack by speaking with his nether mouth, i.e., by farting. The name Eulenspiegel literally means not only "wise mirror," suggestive of his role as a subversive trickster, but also, in Low German, to "wipe one's behind" (Haase, *Greenwood Encyclopedia* 972), which, as I will discuss in detail below, is a motif central to Tawada's "The Bridegroom Was a Dog."

4. Mitsutani's English translation of "The Piper" will be published in *Two Lines: World Writing in Translation* (forthcoming in 2015).

5. To avoid confusion with the title of Anne Duden's text, Tawada later changed the title of her novella from *Arufabetto no kizuguchi* to *Moji ishoku* (Word Transplant).

6. There are also some Japanese tales that end with the transformation of the nonhuman partner into a human being, a happy ending similar to that of Western animal bridegroom tales such as "Beauty and the Beast" and the Grimms' "Hans the Hedgehog." In "Tanishi musuko" (The Mud Snail Son), a rich man's daughter marries a mud snail and lives with him for a while. Her dutifulness is rewarded when her minuscule husband transforms into a handsome—and human-sized—young man. The important difference, however, is that in this Japanese story, in which the specific difference of the nonanimal partner is exaggerated to an absurd extent, the heroine shows no sign of distress at his snailness and carries him around with wifely care.

7. Ozawa's idea here seems to be influenced by the nineteenth-century theories of cultural evolutionism represented by comparative anthropologists such as E. B. Tyler, Andrew Lang, and James Frazer, a view whose binarism seems too reductionist to analyze the complex layering of both Western and non-Western cultures.

8. Fukuda Akira speculates that the reasons why the dog bridegroom tale type was neglected by Yanagita Kunio and his followers might be that Yanagita did not find enough tales belonging to this tale type in Japan and that a similar tale was found in China (36–37).

9. The most widely known version of "Snow Woman" is included in *Kwaidan: Stories and Studies of Strange Things* (1904), a collection of Japanese ghost stories retold by the Greek-born international writer Lafcadio Hearn.

10. In this context, the name Mitsuko can be also connected with the tragic and dutiful beauty in Claude Farrère's novel *La bataille* (1909; The Battle), an Orientalist romance about a British navy officer and his Japanese mistress, Mitsouko, whose name has been widely popularized by the 1919 perfume by Guerlain, said to have been named after Farrère's heroine.

11. It is interesting to note in this connection that the first-person narrator of "A Souvenir of Japan," Angela Carter's semiautobiographical short story, calls her Japanese lover "Taro" (*Fireworks* 5), revealing her own fantasization of their relationship.

12. Although what is inserted into Mitsuko's vagina can be interpreted as either his penis or his tongue in the English translation, the use of the word *mono* (thing) in the Japanese original text leads most readers to make the former interpretation.

13. Katrin Amann points out that Tarō's grandmother's prophecy evokes the curse pronounced at the beginning of *Nansō satomi hakken den* (1814–42; The Chronicles of the Eight Dog Heroes of the Satomi Clan of Nansō), a 106-volume epic novel by Kyokutei [Takizawa] Bakin (1767–1848), the opening chapters of which are based on the dog bridegroom tale. Amann argues that Tawada's text "pornographises" Bakin's work in order to realign the dog bridegroom tale with the premodern narrative structure, which does not exclude the nonhuman (108–10).

CHAPTER 3

1. Ogawa published a series of interviews with Kawai (Ogawa and Kawai) and also mentions Kawai's ideas in her essays.

2. In France, Ogawa's works were first published by Actes Sud, a publisher in Arles renowned for publishing foreign authors so far overlooked in Paris; for example, it introduced to a French readership works by now well-established authors such as Paul Auster, Pat Barker, and W. G. Sebald (Riding).

3. Although Ogawa's "Aisaresugita hakuchō" (The Swan Who Was Loved Too Much), the story of a man who falls in love with a beautiful swan on a lake, seems to draw on *Swan Lake*, Higami's illustrations of a girl and a swan evoke Andersen's "The Wild Swans" as well as the motif of Leda and the Swan from Greek mythology. *Lost and Found Fairy Tales* exemplifies innovative collaborations between writers and artists to create fairy-tale collections in which the text and the image play against, rather than simply explain, each other.

4. Interestingly, Ogawa's emphasis on craftsmanship in a fairy tale finds an echo in Aimee Bender's retelling of "Donkey Skin," collected in Bernheimer's *My Mother She Killed Me, My Father He Ate Me*. Bender's story is told from the perspective of a tailor who makes clothing in the colors of nature. "The Color Master," the title of Bender's story, is also a coined term that is as evocative as Ogawa's titles. Both Ogawa and Bender associate craftsmanship with the art of writing stories and focus on those who dedicate their lives to creating objects that would satisfy their inner needs. Their stories displace the

normative desire for social promotion and heterosexual union in traditional fairy tales and explore a different dimension of desire that can be pursued and fulfilled in fairy tales.

5. For a detailed comparative reading of Andersen's "The Little Mermaid" and Ogawa's "The Life of a Merman Lapidary," see Fraser.

6. My following analysis of *Hotel Iris* draws on the paper I delivered at the Fairy Tale Vanguard Conference held in Ghent, Belgium, in August 2012. I am grateful to the organizers of the conference, Vanessa Joosen and Stijn Praet, and the participants for inspiring exchanges.

7. In her film adaptation of Ogawa's "Specimen of the Ring Finger," Bertrand gives the heroine, who remains unnamed in the original story, the name Iris, which suggests that Bertrand saw the connection between Ogawa's two Bluebeard stories, "Specimen of the Ring Finger" and *Hotel Iris*.

8. See, among others, Bacchilega's analysis of "Bluebeard" in *Postmodern Fairy Tales*.

9. Colleen Shea's "Bluebeard in Japan" gives a comparative reading of *Hotel Iris* and "Bluebeard." Edwin Turner's review also mentions its connection with "Bluebeard."

10. See Vera Mackie's discussion of the mutual dependence of girls' reappropriation of the Lolita figure as a street fashion style and the male fantasy of the Lolita complex in "Reading *Lolita* in Japan."

11. Edwin Turner, for example, describes *Hotel Iris* as "reverse-*Lolita*."

12. The topographical liminality connects Ogawa's novel to Carter's "The Bloody Chamber," which is also set on a tidal island in Brittany. Although, unlike Carter, Ogawa seems unaware of Brittany's association with various historical Bluebeard-like figures, such as Gilles de Rais and Cunmar the Accursed, this in-between setting—between land and sea—plays an important symbolic role in Ogawa's story as it does in Carter's.

CHAPTER 4

1. The job of operating elevators existed in other countries as well, but with the disappearance of manually operated elevators in the 1960s, the job has become almost obsolete except in Japan and Taiwan.

2. Yuka's bright red hair, indicating her rebellious, punkish spirit, may also be a reference to the female demons in the tradition of Noh theater, who are sometimes depicted with shaggy long hair in bright red just like Yuka's.

3. Yanagi herself made this point clear in a letter to David Elliott: "Anyone who wants to represent themselves as a grandmother fifty years later is OK, without age limits (presently there are 'grandmothers' from twelve to forty-five years of age), of any nationality. They can even be men as long as they imagine themselves as a grandmother" (*Miwa Yanagi* 72).

4. Matsumoto Leiji states that *Ginga tetsudō 999* was inspired by Maurice Maeterlinck's play *The Blue Bird* (1908)—the name Maetel seems to be derived from Maeterlinck—and Miyazawa Kenji's children's story *Ginga tetsudō no yoru* (1934; Night on the Galactic Railroad).

5. I am grateful to the anonymous reviewer at Wayne State University Press for drawing my attention to this connection.

6. Yanagi herself points out the influence of both Abe's and Márquez's works depicting women associated with sand on her image of Sand Woman in her self-staged conversation between herself and a fictional female writer (*Fairy Tale* 69).

7. In "Fiction and Its Phantoms: A Reading of Freud's *Das Unheimliche* (The 'Uncanny')," Hélène Cixous argues that the womb figures as a radical duplicity in Freud's "The Uncanny" as Freud's overlooking of the figure of the doll exposes a gap in the unity of reality where death enters as the Other of life.

8. Reassuringly enough, Márquez's story tells us that the grandmother does not die even after eating the whole cake. Yanagi states that it was Eréndira's grandmother, "an extremely wicked, immortal being with powerful fixations on life and sexuality, a really grotesque creature," that she had in her mind as a kind of ur-grandmother for her My Grandmothers series (*Fairy Tale* 70).

9. Smith's *Sleeping Witch* appears on the cover of Helaine Posner and Smith's *Kiki Smith: Telling Tales*.

10. For other variants of the tale, see Sasama.

11. The ambiguous figure of a yamauba can be seen as having a closer kinship with a Baba Yaga in Russian fairy tales than with witches in west European tales. In *Baba Yaga: The Ambiguous Mother and Witch of the Russian Folktale*, Andreas Johns analyzes the fundamental ambiguity of this figure whose functions are neither purely benevolent nor purely hostile. Johns's description of a Baba Yaga also seems to apply to a yamauba: "Baba Yaga is a liminal, borderline character, mediating between human and supernatural, human and nonhuman. . . . [S]he also mediates the oppositions of male/female, own/foreign, Self/Other, and, of course, nature and culture" (271). Johns also states that "Baba Yaga's ambiguity logically reflects the human relationship to nature, which is fundamentally ambivalent" (273). Although her tumbledown hut may look less striking than a Baba Yaga's, a yamauba, like her Russian sister, is a Mother Earth figure endowed with a contradictory nature and supernatural power.

12. The outlines of "Ushikata to yamauba," "Ubakawa," and "Yamauba to nakōdo" are based on *Nihon mukashibanasi taisei* (Seki et al.). Selected tales edited by Seki are translated into English by Robert J. Adams as *Folktales of Japan* (1963).

13. The mythologist Yoshida Atsuhiko relates the yamauba figure to various female deities in Japanese mythology who produce food from different parts of their bodies (108–12). The two goddesses of food in Japanese mythology,

Ōgetsu-hime and Ukemochi-no-kami (their names mean "a goddess of abundant food" and "a goddess who possesses food," respectively), both keep producing various kinds of food from their bodies even after their death. S. Yumiko Hulvey's "Myths and Monsters: The Female Body as the Site for Political Agendas" explores the relationship between the yamauba topos and the female deities in the Japanese creation myth.

14. Royall Tyler's English translation of *Yamamba* is included in *Japanese Nō Dramas*.

15. These are both often-quoted phrases from the *Han'nya shinkyō* (Heart Sutra), the best-known Buddhist scripture.

16. In some folktales, a yamauba is killed by stones. In a tale called "Yamauba to ishimochi" (Mountain Witch and Stone Cake), for example, the yamauba is tricked into eating stones and dies, evoking the Grimms' "The Wolf and the Seven Young Kids" and "Little Red Riding Hood," in which the wolf dies of having his belly stuffed with stones. The yamauba in these tales can be seen as an allomotif of the wolf in European tales.

17. This destabilizing juxtaposition of the desire to indulge in a fantasy arising from one's deep psyche with the urge to pull away and regard it from the outside is also the strategy Carter uses in her feminist rewriting of fairy tales in *The Bloody Chamber*.

18. This episode recalls a Baba Yaga's transgression of the roles of the two generations in the Russian tale "The Bull Savior" (the East Slavic tale-type index 314A*), in which she forces the girl to sing her a lullaby or rock her to sleep. See Johns (131–32).

19. A skyscraper rooftop often functions as a liminal space in contemporary visual culture, such as in sci-fi films where heroes and villains fight the age-old battle between good and evil.

CHAPTER 5

1. For a discussion of the role of foxes in Ōe no Masafusa's *Kobiki* (Fox-Haunting Record), see Li (193–94).

2. Personal correspondence with the author.

3. Hello Kitty is a white female kitten wearing a red ribbon created by the Japanese company Sanrio in 1974. Hello Kitty is arguably the most famous icon of kawaii, the Japanese aesthetic of cuteness.

4. The most conspicuous example of this approach is arguably Ruth B. Bottigheimer's *Fairy Tale: A New History*, whose "author-centered and European-centered" approach to the history of fairy tales has been criticized by such

critics as Bacchilega, Dan Ben-Amos, and Zipes (Bacchilega, *Fairy Tales Transformed?* 200).

EPILOGUE

1. See, for example, Beckett (*Red Riding Hood for All Ages* 81–84, 209–10); Cavallaro; Ortabasi; Shamoon; Duggan (103–39); Missiou; and Murai ("Guro-Kawaii").

2. Kobayashi Fumihiko's *Japanese Animal-Wife Tales: Narrating Gender Reality in Japanese Folktale Tradition* (2014) was published while I was finalizing the manuscript of this book; unfortunately, I was unable to benefit from Kobayashi's excellent study on this tale type in Japan.

WORKS CITED

Amann, Katrin. *Yugamu shintai: Gendai sakka no henshintan* [Bodies That Distort: Stories of Transformation by Contemporary Writers]. Tokyo: Senshū Daigaku Shuppankyoku, 2000. Print.

L'annulaire. Dir. Diane Bertrand. Screenplay by Diane Bertrand. Memento Films, 2005. Film.

Antoni, Klaus. "Momotarō (The Peach Boy) and the Spirit of Japan: Concerning the Function of a Fairy Tale in Japanese Nationalism of the Early Showa Age." *Asian Folklore Studies* 50 (1991): 155–88. Print.

Aoyama, Tomoko, and Barbara Hartley, eds. *Girl Reading Girl in Japan*. London: Routledge, 2010. Print.

Atwood, Margaret. "Running with the Tigers." *Flesh and the Mirror: Essays on the Art of Angela Carter*. Ed. Lorna Sage. London: Virago, 1994. 117–35. Print.

Ayame, Hiroharu. *Ogawa Yōko: Mienai sekai o mitsumete*. Tokyo: Bensei Shuppan, 2009. Print.

Baba, Akiko. *Baba Akiko kashū*. Gendai kajin bunko 15. Tokyo: Kokubunsha, 1978. Print.

Bacchilega, Cristina. *Fairy Tales Transformed? Twenty-First-Century Adaptations and the Politics of Wonder*. Detroit: Wayne State UP, 2013. Print.

———. *Postmodern Fairy Tales: Gender and Narrative Strategies*. Philadelphia: U of Pennsylvania P, 1997. Print.

———. "Whetting Her Appetite: What's a 'Clever' Woman to Do in the Grimms' Collection?" Turner and Greenhill 27–47. Print.

Beckett, Sandra L. *Red Riding Hood for All Ages: A Fairy-Tale Icon in Cross-Cultural Contexts*. Detroit: Wayne State UP, 2008. Print.

———. *Revisioning Red Riding Hood around the World: An Anthology of International Retellings*. Detroit: Wayne State UP, 2014. Print.

Benjamin, Walter. *Illuminations*. 1955. Trans. Harry Zohn. Ed. Hannah Arendt. New York: Harcourt Brace Jovanovich, 1968. Print.

Benson, Stephen, ed. *Contemporary Fiction and the Fairy Tale*. Detroit: Wayne State UP, 2008. Print.

Bernheimer, Kate, ed. *My Mother She Killed Me, My Father He Ate Me: Forty New Fairy Tales*. New York: Penguin, 2010. Print.

Betsuyaku, Minoru. *The Little Match Girl*. Trans. Robert N. Lawson. *The Columbia Anthology of Modern Japanese Literature: From 1945 to the Present*. Ed. J. Thomas Rimer and Van C. Gessel. New York: Columbia UP, 2007. 452–75. Print.

Bishop, Stephanie. "Besotted with Pain." *Times Literary Supplement* 18 June 2010. Web. 22 Sep. 2014.

Bonner, Sarah. "Visualising Little Red Riding Hood." *Movable Type* 2 (2006). Web. 1 July 2009.

Bottigheimer, Ruth B. *Fairy Tales: A New History*. Albany: State U of New York P, 2009. Print.

Buckley, Sandra. *Broken Silence: Voices of Japanese Feminism*. Berkley: U of California P, 1997. Print.

Cardi, Luciana. "'A Fool Will Never Be Happy': Kurahashi Yumiko's Retelling of 'Snow White.'" *Marvels & Tales: Journal of Fairy-Tale Studies* 27.2 (2013): 194–204. Print.

Carter, Angela. 1976. "The Better to Eat You With." *Shaking a Leg: Journalism and Writings*. Ed. Jenny Uglow. London: Vintage, 1998. 451–55. Print.

———. *The Bloody Chamber and Other Stories*. London: Gollancz, 1979. Print.

———. *Fireworks: Nine Profane Pieces*. 1974. London: Virago, 1988. Print.

———. *The Sadeian Woman: An Exercise in Cultural History*. London: Virago, 1979. Print.

Cavallaro, Dani. *The Fairy Tale and Anime: Traditional Themes, Images, and Symbols at Play on Screen*. Jefferson, NC: McFarland, 2011. Print.

Charles, Ron. "Infinite Loop." Rev. of *The Housekeeper and the Professor*, by Ogawa Yōko. *Washington Post* 15 Feb. 2009. Web. 22 Sep. 2014.

Cininas, Jazmina. "The Girlie Werewolf Hall of Fame: Historical and Contemporary Figurations of the Female Lycanthrope." Diss. Royal Melbourne Institute of Technology, 2013. Web. 22 Sep. 2014.

Cixous, Hélène. "Fiction and Its Phantoms: A Reading of Freud's *Das Unheimliche* (The 'Uncanny')." *New Literary History* 7 (1976): 525–48. Print.

The Company of Wolves. Dir. Neil Jordan. Screenplay by Neil Jordan and Angela Carter. Incorporated Television Company, 1984. Film.

Damrosch, David. "Comparing the Incomparable: World Literature from Du Fu to Mishima." *Renixa* 3 (2012): 133–55. Web. 22 Sep. 2014.

———. *What Is World Literature?* Princeton: Princeton UP, 2003. Print.

Davis, Jason, and Mio Bryce. "I Love You as You Are: Marriages between Different Kinds." *International Journal of Diversity in Organisations, Communities and Nations* 7.6 (2008): 201–10. Print.

de Beaumont, Jeanne-Marie Leprince. "Beauty and the Beast." *The Classic Fairy Tales*. Ed. Iona Opie and Peter Opie. London: Oxford UP, 1974. 182–95. Print.

de Beaumont, Jeanne-Marie Leprince, et al. *Seiyō senkyō kidan*. Trans. Inoue Kan'ichi. Tokyo: Tōyōdō, 1896. Print.

de Lauretis, Teresa. *Alice Doesn't: Feminism, Semiotics, Cinema*. Bloomington: Indiana UP, 1984. Print.

Dower, John D. *War without Mercy: Race and Power in the Pacific War*. New York: Pantheon, 1986. Print.

Dowling, Colette. *The Cinderella Complex: Women's Hidden Fear of Independence*. New York: Summit, 1981. Print.

Duggan, Anne E. *Queer Enchantments: Gender, Sexuality, and Class in the Fairy-Tale Cinema of Jacques Demy*. Detroit: Wayne State UP, 2014. Print.

Fraser, Lucy. "Lost Property Fairy Tales: Ogawa Yōko and Higami Kumiko's Transformations of 'The Little Mermaid.'" *Marvels & Tales: Journal of Fairy-Tale Studies* 27.2 (2013): 181–93. Print.

Freud, Sigmund. "From the History of an Infantile Neurosis [The 'Wolfman']." 1918. *The "Wolfman" and Other Cases*. Harmondsworth, UK: Penguin, 2002. 203–320. Print.

———. "The Theme of the Three Caskets." 1913. *Art and Literature*. Trans. James Strachey. Ed. Angela Richards and Albert Dickson. The Penguin Freud Library, vol. 14. Harmondsworth, UK: Penguin, 1990 233–47. Print.

———. "The Uncanny." 1919. *The Uncanny*. Trans. David McLintock. London: Penguin, 2003. 123–62. Print.

Fujikawa, Yoshiyuki. Afterword to *Chizome no heya: Otona no tame no gensō dōwa* [The Bloody Chamber], by Angela Carter. Trans. Fujikawa Yoshiyuki. Tokyo: Chikumashobō, 1992. 253–67.

Fukawa, Gen'ichirō. "Anderusen dōwa to Gurimu dōwa no honpō shoyaku o megutte [On the First Translations of Andersen's Tales and Grimms' Tales in Japan]." *Bungaku* 9.4 (2008) 140–51. Print.

Fuku, Noriko, and Christopher Phillips, eds. *Heavy Light: Recent Photography and Video from Japan*. New York: International Center of Photography; Göttingen: Steidl, 2008. Print.

Fukuda, Akira. "Inumukoiri no denshō." *Mukashibanashi: Kenkyū to shiryō 4*. Ed. Mukashibanashi Konwa-kai. Tokyo: Miyai Shoten, 1975. 36–69. Print.

Fuse, Hideto. "Kaisetsu." Ogawa. *Kusuriyubi no hyōhon*, 181–85. Print.

Galchen, Rivka. "Yoko Tawada's Magnificent Strangeness." *New Yorker* 19 Oct. 2012. Web. 22 Sep. 2014.

Gilbert, Sandra M., and Susan Gubar. *The Mad Woman in the Attic: The Woman Writer and the Nineteenth-Century Literary Imagination*. New Haven: Yale UP, 1979. Print.

Grimm, Jacob, and Wilhelm Grimm. *The Complete Fairy Tales.* Trans. Jack Zipes. London: Vintage, 2007.

———. "Koyukihime." Trans. Iwaya Sazanami. *Shōnen sekai* 2.8 (1896): 25–29. Print.

Haase, Donald. *Fairy Tales and Feminism: New Approaches.* Detroit: Wayne State UP, 2004. Print.

———, ed. *The Greenwood Encyclopedia of Folktales and Fairy Tales.* Westport, CT: Greenwood, 2008. Print.

Haffenden, John. "Angela Carter." *Novelists in Interview.* London: Methuen, 1985. 76–96. Print.

Hearn, Lafcadio. *Kwaidan: Stories and Studies of Strange Things.* Boston: Houghton Mifflin, 1904. Print.

Hennard Dutheil de la Rochère, Martine. "Updating the Politics of Experience: Angela Carter's Translation of Charles Perrault's 'Le petit chaperon rouge.'" *Palimpsestes* 22 (2009): 187–204. Web. 22 Sep. 2014.

Hoffmann, E. T. A., "The Sandman." 1816. *Tales of Hoffmann.* Ed. and trans. R. J. Hollingdale. Harmondsworth, UK: Penguin, 1982. 85–125. Print.

Honda, Masuko. "The Genealogy of *Hirahira*: Liminality and the Girl." Aoyama and Hartley 19–37. Print.

Hoogland, Cornelia. *Woods Wolf Girl.* Hamilton, Ontario: Wolsak and Wynn, 2011. Print.

Rev. of *Hotel Iris,* by Ogawa Yōko. *Kirkus Reviews* 15 Mar. 2010: 225. Print.

Hulvey, S. Yumiko. "Myths and Monsters: The Female Body as the Site for Political Agendas." *Body Politics and the Fictional Double.* Ed. Debra Walker King. Bloomington: Indiana UP, 2000. 71–88. Print.

Ikeda, Kayoko. "Gurimu kenkyūsha kara mita *Hontō wa Osoroshii* . . . Tōyōmondai [The Problem of Plagiarism in *Grimms' Tales Really Are Horrific* Seen from a Grimm Scholar's Perspective]. *Tsukuru* 29.11 (1999): 76–79. Print.

Ikeda, Riyoko. *Berusaiyu no bara.* 5 vols. 1972–73. Tokyo: Shūeisha, 1994. Print.

Ikoma, Natsumi. *Yokubō suru bungaku: Odoru kyōjo de yomitoku nichiei jendā hihyō.* Tokyo: Eihōsha, 2007. Print.

Itō, Kanako. "'Hitotsuya' kō: Utagawa Kuniyoshi o chūshin ni" [On "A Lonely House," with Emphasis on Kuniyoshi Utagawa's Work]. *Geisou: Tsukuba Daigaku geijutsugaku kenkyūshi* 21 (2004): 35–64. Print.

Izumi, Kyōka. "Kōya hijiri." 1900. *Kōya hijiri.* Tokyo: Iwanami Shoten, 1936. 5–85. Print.

Johns, Andreas. *Baba Yaga: The Ambiguous Mother and Witch of the Russian Folktale.* New York: Peter Lang, 2004. Print.

Joosen, Vanessa. *Critical and Creative Perspectives on Fairy Tales: An Intertextual Dialogue between Fairy-Tale Scholarship and Postmodern Retellings.* Detroit: Wayne State UP, 2011. Print.

Kaguya-hime no monogatari. Dir. Takahata Isao. Studio Ghibli, 2013. Film.

Kaneda, Kiichi, trans. *Gurimu dōwa shū.* 2 vols. *Sekai dōwa taikei* 2 and 23. Tokyo: Iwanami Bunko, 1924, 1927. Print.

Kawabata, Yasunari. *House of the Sleeping Beauties and Other Stories.* Trans. Edward G. Seidensticker. Tokyo: Kodansha International, 1969. Print.

———. *Nemureru bijo.* Tokyo: Shinchōsha, 1961. Print.

Kawahara, Kazue. *Kodomokan no kindai:* Akai Tori *to "dōshin" no risō* [The Concept of the Child in the Modern Era: *Red Bird* and the Ideal of "Children's Minds"]. Tokyo: Chūōkōron Shinsha, 1998. Print.

Kawai, Hayao. *The Japanese Psyche: Major Motifs in the Fairy Tales of Japan.* 1988. Trans. Kawai Hayao and Sachiko Reece. Woodstock: Spring, 1996. Print.

———. *Mukashibanashi to nihonjin no kokoro.* Tokyo, Iwanami Shoten, 1982. Print.

Kim, Jong Bom. "*Konjaku monogatarishū* nimiru Chōsen kankei setsuwa shōkō." *Kokubungaku: Kaishaku to kanshō.* 57.5 (1992): 168–75. Print.

Kinoshita, Junji. *Yūzuru.* 1949. *Kinoshita Junji shū 1.* Tokyo: Iwanami Shoten, 1988. 1–42. Print.

———. *Twilight Crane.* Trans. A. C. Scott. *Playbook: Five Plays for a New Theatre.* New York: New Directions, 1956. 131–59. Print.

Kinsella, Sharon. "Cuties in Japan." *Women, Media and Consumption in Japan.* Ed. Lise Skov and Brian Moeran. Honolulu: U of Hawai'i P. 220–54. Print.

Kiryū, Misao. *Hontō wa osoroshii Gurimu dōwa.* Tokyo: KK Bestsellers, 1998. Print.

Kōnoike, Tomoko. *Inter-traveller: People Playing with the Dead.* Tokyo: Hatori Shoten, 2009. Print.

———. "Intabyū: Kōnoike Tomoko." Interview by Saitō Tamaki. *Bijutsu techō* 57 (2005): 21–25. Print.

———. *Mimio.* Tokyo: Seigensha, 2001. Print.

Kotani, Mari. "Kaisetsu: Yajū no tsumi to bijo no batsu." Afterword to *Chizome no heya: Otona no tame no gensō dōwa* [*The Bloody Chamber*], by Angela Carter. Trans. Fujikawa Yoshiyuki. Rev. ed. Tokyo: Chikumashobō, 1999. 305–9. Print.

Kudō, Yōko, ed. and trans. *Ima yomu Perō "Mukashibanashi"* [Reading Perrault's *Contes du temps passé* Now]. Cover art by Kōnoike Tomoko. Tokyo: Hatori Shoten, 2013. Print.

Kurahashi, Yumiko. *Otona no tame no zankoku dōwa.* Tokyo: Shinchōsha, 1984. Print.

Li, Michelle Osterfeld. *Ambiguous Bodies: Reading the Grotesque in Japanese Setsuwa Tales.* Stanford: Stanford UP, 2009. Print.

Lieberman, Marcia K. "Some Day My Prince Will Come: Female Acculturation through the Fairy Tale." 1972. *Don't Bet on the Prince: Contemporary*

Feminist Fairy Tales in North America and England. Ed. Jack Zipes. 1986. New York: Routledge, 1989. 185–200. Print.

Lüthi, Max. *The European Folktale: Form and Nature.* 1947. Trans. John D. Niles. Bloomington: Indiana UP, 1986. Print.

Mabuchi, Kazuo, et al., eds. *Konjaku monogatarishū.* Nihon koten bungaku zenshū 24. Tokyo: Shōgakukan, 1976. Print.

Mackie, Vera. "Reading Lolita in Japan." Aoyama and Hartley, 187–201. Print.

Maitland, Sara. *Gossip from the Forest: The Tangled Roots of Our Forests and Fairytales.* London: Granta, 2012. Print.

Márquez, Gabriel García. "The Incredible and Sad Tale of Innocent Eréndira and Her Heartless Grandmother." 1972. *Innocent Eréndira and Other Stories.* Trans. Gregory Rabassa. London: Penguin, 1996. Print.

Maruyama, Noboru. "*Hontō wa osoroshii Gurimu dōwa* tōyō-mondai, hōtei e!?" [The Problem of Plagiarism in *Grimms' Tales Really Are Horrific* Goes to Court?] *Tsukuru* 29.11 (1999): 68–75. Print.

Matsumoto, Leiji. *Ginga testudō 999.* 18 vols. 1977–87. Tokyo: Shōnengahō-sha, 1994. Print.

Matsumoto, Yūko. *Tsumibukai hime no otogibanashi.* Tokyo: Kadokawa Shoten, 1996. Print.

Mills, Douglas Edgar, trans. *A Collection of Tales from Uji: A Study and Translation of Uji Shūi Monogatari.* University of Cambridge Oriental Publications 15. Cambridge: Cambridge UP, 1970. Print.

Missiou, Marianna. "Retelling 'Hansel and Gretel' in Comic Book and Manga Narration: The Case of Philip Petit and Mizuno Junko." *Grimms' Tales around the Globe: The Dynamics of Their International Reception.* Ed. Vanessa Joosen and Gillian Lathey. Detroit: Wayne State UP, 2014. 257–74. Print.

Mitsutani, Margaret. "Tawada Yōko's 'The Man with Two Mouths.'" *Marvels & Tales: Journal of Fairy-Tale Studies* 27.2 (2013): 321–29. Print.

———. "Translator's Afterword." *Facing the Bridge*, by Tawada Yōko, trans. Margaret Mitsutani. New York: New Directions, 2007. 176–86. Print.

Mizuta, Noriko, and Kitada Sachie, eds. *Yamambatachi no monogatari: Josei no genkei to katarinaoshi.* Tokyo: Gakugei Shorin, 2002. Print.

Murai, Mayako. "Before and After the 'Grimm Boom': Re-interpretations of Grimm's Tales in Contemporary Japan." *Grimms' Tales around the Globe: The Dynamics of Their International Reception.* Ed. Vanessa Joosen and Gillian Lathey. Detroit: Wayne State UP, 2014. 153–76. Print.

———. "Bluebeard in Contemporary Japanese Fiction: Yoko Ogawa's *Hotel Iris.*" Fairy Tale Vanguard Conference. Ghent, Belgium. 20–22 Aug. 2012. Address.

———. "Guro-Kawaii Re-envisionings of Fairy Tales in Contemporary Japanese Art." *Postmodern Reinterpretations of Fairy Tales: How Applying New*

Methods Generates New Meanings. Ed. Anna Kérchy. New York: Edwin Mellen, 2011. 145–62. Print.

———. "In the Midst of Metamorphosis: Yōko Tawada's 'The Bridegroom Was a Dog.'" *New Fairy Tales: Essays and Stories.* Ed. John Patrick Pazdziora and Defne Çizakça. Oklahoma City: Unlocking, 2013. 281–97. Print.

———. "In the Realm of the Senses: Tomoko Konoike's Visual Recasting of 'Little Red Riding Hood.'" *Anti-tales: The Uses of Disenchantment.* Ed. Catriona Fay McAra and David Calvin. Newcastle: Cambridge Scholars, 2011. 152–62. Print.

———. "The Princess, the Witch, and the Fireside: Yanagi Miwa's Uncanny Restaging of Fairy Tales." *Marvels & Tales: Journal of Fairy-Tale Studies* 27.2 (2013): 234–53. Print.

———. "The Translation and Reception of Angela Carter's Work in Japan." *Angela Carter traductrice—Angela Carter en traduction.* Ed. Martine Hennard Dutheil de la Rochère. Cahiers du Centre de Traduction Littéraire 56. Lausanne: Centre de Traduction Littéraire, 2014. 39–55. Print.

Nagura, Yōko. *Nihon no kindaika to Gurimu dōwa: Jidai ni yoru henka o yomitoku* [Japan's Modernization and the Grimms' Tales: Interpreting the Changes over Time]. Tokyo: Sekaishisōsha, 2005. Print.

Nochlin, Linda. "Black, White, and Uncanny: Miwa Yanagi's Fairy Tale." Fuku and Phillips 232–41. Print.

Noguchi, Yoshiko. "Eiyakubon kara jūyaku sareta nihon no Gurimu dōwa: Saisho no hōyakubon o chūshin ni [Grimms' Fairy Tales Translated from the English in Japan: Focusing on the First Japanese Translation]. *Jidō bungaku hon'yaku sakuhin sōran* 4. Ed. Kawato Michiaki and Sakakibara Takanori. Tokyo: Nada Shuppan Center, 2005. 465–85. Print.

———. *Gurimu no meruhyen: Sono yume to genjitsu* [Grimms' Märchen: Dream and Reality]. Tokyo: Keisō Shobō, 1994. Print.

Ogawa, Yōko. "Chūgoku yasai no sodatekata." *Mabuta.* Tokyo: Shinchōsha, 2001. 31–54. Print.

———. *The Diving Pool.* 2008. Trans. Stephen Synder. London: Vintage, 2009. Print.

———. "Domitorī." 1990. *Ninshin karendā.* Tokyo: Bungei Shunjū, 1994. 75–148. Print.

———. *Fukaki kokoro no soko yori* [From the Depths of the Mind]. 1999. Tokyo: PHP Kenkyūsho, 2006. Print.

———. *Hakase no aishita sūshiki.* Tokyo: Shinchōsha, 2003. Print.

———. *Hisoyakana kessyō.* Tokyo: Kōdansha, 1994. Print.

———. *Hotel Iris.* Trans. Stephen Synder. 2010. London: Vintage, 2011. Print.

———. *Hoteru airisu.* Tokyo: Gakusyū-kenkyūsha, 1996. Print.

———. *The Housekeeper and the Professor.* 2009. Trans. Stephen Snyder. London: Vintage, 2010. Print.

———. "Kusuriyubi no hyōhon." 1992. *Kusuriyubi no hyōhon.* Tokyo: Shinchōsha, 1994. 7–90. Print.

———. "Ninshin karendā." 1990. *Ninshin karendā.* Tokyo: Bungei Shunjū, 1994. 7–74. Print.

———. *Otogibanashi no wasuremono.* Illus. Higami Kumiko. Tokyo: HOME-SHA, 2006. Print.

———. *Revenge: Eleven Dark Tales.* Trans. Stephen Snyder. London: Harvill Secker, 2013. Print.

———. "Samenai kōcha." 1990. *Kanpekina byōshitsu.* Tokyo: Chūōkōron-Shinsha, 2004. 133–88. Print.

Ogawa, Yōko, and Kawai Hayao. *Ikiru towa jibun no monogatari o tsukurukoto* [To Live Is to Create Your Own Story]. Tokyo: Shinchōsha, 2008. Print.

Orenstein, Catherine. *Little Red Riding Hood Uncloaked: Sex, Morality, and the Evolution of a Fairy Tale.* New York: Basic, 2002. Print.

Ortabasi, Melek. "(Re)animating Folklore: Raccoon Dogs, Foxes, and Other Supernatural Japanese Citizens in Takahata Isao's *Heisei tanuki gassen pompoko.*" *Marvels & Tales: Journal of Fairy-Tale Studies* 27.2 (2013): 254–75. Print.

Ozawa, Toshio. *Mukashibanashi no kosumorojī: Hito to dōbutsu tono kon'intan.* Tokyo: Kōdansha, 1994. Print.

Ozawa, Toshio, et al., eds. *Gendai ni ikiru Gurimu.* Tokyo: Iwanami Shoten, 1985. Print.

Perrault, Charles. *Nagagutsu o haita neko* (Puss in Boots). Trans. Shibusawa Tatsuhiko. Tokyo: Daiwa Shōbo, 1973. Print.

Posner, Helaine, and Kiki Smith. *Kiki Smith: Telling Tales.* New York: International Center of Photography, 2001. Print.

Propp, Vladimir. *Morphology of the Folktale.* 1928. Trans. Laurence Scott. Austin: U of Texas P, 1968. Print.

Riding, Alan. "French House Flourishes on Publishing Periphery." *New York Times* 28 Apr. 2005. Web. 22 Sep. 2014.

Sakai, Cécile. "Hon'yaku no rikigaku: Nihon bungaku no furansugo yaku nitsuite [The Dynamics of Translation: On the French Translation of Japanese Literature]. *Gengo Bunka* 22 (Mar. 2005): 88–117. Print.

Sakamoto, Rieko. "Riaru wārudo: Sekai no hadazawari [Real World: World Senses]. *Rokumori miraizu.* Ed. Kōnoike Tomoko et al. Tokyo: Mori Art Museum, 44–47. Print.

Sakuraba, Kazuki. *Fuse: Gansaku Satomi hakkenden.* Illus. Kōnoike Tomoko. Tokyo: Bungei Shunjū, 2010. Print.

Sano, Yōko. *Uso bakka: Shinshaku sekai otogibanashi.* 1985. Tokyo: Kōdansha, 1998. Print.

Sasama, Yoshihiko. *Oni-onna densyō to sono minzoku: Hitotsuya monogatari no sekai* [Legends and Folklore about Ogresses: The World of the Story of a Lonely House]. Tokyo: Yūzankaku, 1992. Print.

Seki, Keigo, et al., eds. *Nihon mukashibanashi taisei.* 12 vols. Tokyo: Kadokawa Shoten, 1978–80. Print.

Sexton, Anne. *Transformations.* Boston: Houghton and Mifflin, 1971. Print.

Shamoon, Deborah. "The Yōkai in the Database: Supernatural Creatures and Folklore in Manga and Anime." *Marvels & Tales: Journal of Fairy-Tale Studies* 27.2 (2013): 276–89. Print.

Shea, Colleen. "Bluebeard in Japan." Rev. of *Hotel Iris,* by Ogawa Yōko. *Open Letters Monthly: An Arts and Literature Review* 9 Aug. 2012. Web. 22 Sep. 2014.

Shibusawa, Tatsuhiko. *Erotishizumu.* 1967. Tokyo: Chūōkōron-sha, 1996. Print.

———. *Kobiki.* 1982. Cover art by Kōnoike Tomoko. Tokyo: Heibonsha, 2004. Print.

Slaymaker, Doug, ed. *Yōko Tawada: Voices from Everywhere.* Lanham, MD: Lexington, 2007. Print.

Snyder, Stephen. "Two Voices: Stephen Snyder on Yoko Ogawa, Haruki Murakami, and the Business of International Literature." Recording of a lecture given on 10 May 2011 and uploaded on 12 May 2011. The Center for the Art of Translation. Web. 22 Sep. 2014.

Steven, Ridgely C. "Terayama Shūji and Bluebeard." *Marvels & Tales: Journal of Fairy-Tale Studies* 27.2 (2103): 290–300. Print.

Suga, Ryōhō. *Seiyō koji: Shinsen sōwa.* Tokyo: Shūseisha, 1887. Print.

Sugita, Hideaki. "The *Arabian Nights* in Modern Japan: A Brief Historical Sketch." *The Arabian Nights and Orientalism: Perspectives from East and West.* Ed. Yamanaka Yuriko and Nishio Tetsuo. London: Tauris, 116–53. Print.

Suzuki, Shō. *Gurimu dōwa: Meruhen no shinsō.* Tokyo: Kōdansha, 1991. Print.

Tani, Atara, and Okamoto Yasuaki, eds. *Ima iru tokoro/Ima aru watashi: VOCA ni utsushidasareta gendai.* Utsunomiya: Utsunomiya Museum of Art, 2007. Print.

Tanizaki, Jun'ichirō. "Ningyo no nageki." 1917. *Ningyo no nageki, Majutsushi.* Tokyo: Chūōkōron-Shinsha, 1978. 7–51. Print.

———. *Shunkin shō.* 1933. Tokyo: Shinchōsha, 1951. Print.

Tatar, Maria *The Hard Facts of the Grimms' Fairy Tales.* 2nd ed. Princeton: Princeton UP, 2003. Print.

———. *Secrets beyond the Door: The Story of Bluebeard and His Wives.* Princeton: Princeton UP, 2004. Print.

Tawada, Yōko. *Arufabetto no kizuguchi.* Tokyo: Kawade Shobō Shinsha, 1993. Print.

———. "The Bridegroom Was a Dog." *The Bridegroom Was a Dog.* Trans. Margaret Mitsutani. Tokyo: Kodansha International, 2003. 7–62. Print.

———. "A Conversation with Yoko Tawada: Professor Amir Eshel of Stanford University Talks with Author Yoko Tawada about Her Work." 18 Feb. 2009. Web. 22 Sep. 2014.

———. *Facing the Bridge*. Trans. and with an afterword by Margaret Mitsutani. New York: New Directions, 2007. Print.

———. *Futakuchi otoko*. Tokyo: Kawade Shobō Shinsha. 1998. Print.

———. "Inumukoiri." *Inumukoiri*. Tokyo: Kōdansha, 1993. 77–137. Print.

———. "Kakato o nakushite." *Sannin kankei*. Tokyo: Kōdansha, 1992. 7–81. Print.

———. *Katakoto no uwagoto* [Raving in Broken Language]. Tokyo: Seidosha, 2007. Print.

———. *Yoru hikaru tsuru no kamen*. *Shiatā ātsu* 2 (May 1996): 182–99. Print.

———. *Where Europe Begins*. Trans. Susan Bernofsky and Yumi Selden. New York: New Directions, 2002. Print.

Turner, Edwin. Rev. of *Hotel Iris,* by Ogawa Yōko. *biblioklept* 4 May 2010. Web. 22 Sep. 2014.

Turner, Kay. "Playing with Fire: Transgression as Truth in Grimms' 'Frau Trude.'" Turner and Greenhill 245–74. Print.

Turner, Kay, and Pauline Greenhill, eds. *Transgressive Tales: Queering the Grimms*. Detroit: Wayne State UP, 2012. Print.

Ueno, Chizuko. "Miwa Yanagi." *Miwa Yanagi.* Ed. Deutsche Bank Art. Frankfurt: Hatje Cantz, 2004. 61–65. Print.

Ury, Marian, trans. *Tales of Times Now Past: Sixty-Two Stories from a Medieval Japanese Collection*. Berkley: U of California P, 1979. Print.

Viswanathan, Meera. "In Pursuit of the *Yamamba*: The Question of Female Resistance." *The Woman's Hand: Gender and Theory in Japanese Women's Writing*. Ed. Paul Gordon Schalow and Janet A. Walker. Stanford: Stanford UP, 1995. 239–61. Print.

Warner, Marina. *From the Beast to the Blonde: On Fairy Tales and Their Tellers*. 1994. London: Vintage, 1995. Print.

———. "Wolf-Girl, Soul-Bird: The Mortal Art of Kiki Smith." *Kiki Smith: A Gathering, 1980–2005*. Siri Engberg, with contributions by Linda Nochlin, Linne Tillman, and Marina Warner. Minneapolis: Walker Art Center, 2005. 42–53. Print.

Watanabe, Manabu. Rev. of *Mukashibanashi to nihonjin no kokoro,* by Kawai Hayao. *Japanese Journal of Religious Studies* 10.4 (1983): 329–32. Print.

Wilson, Michiko N. "Ōba Minako the Raconteur: Refashioning a *Yamauba* Tale." *Marvels & Tales: Journal of Fairy-Tale Studies* 27.2 (2013): 218–33. Print.

The Wizard of Oz. Dir. Victor Fleming. Metro-Goldwyn-Mayer, 1939. Film.

Yanagi, Miwa. *Elevator Girls*. Kyoto: Seigensha, 2007. Print.

———. *Fairy Tale: Strange Stories of Women Young and Old*. Kyoto: Seigensha, 2007. Print.

———. "Miwa Yanagi." Interview by Wakasa Mako. *Journal of Contemporary Art* 19 Aug. 2001. Web. 22 Sep. 2014.

———. *Miwa Yanagi*. Kyoto: Tankōsha, 2009. Print.

———. "A Supremely Comfortable Place to Be." Interview by Christopher Phillips. Trans. Eric C. Shiner. Fuku and Phillips 212–21. Print.

Yanagita, Kunio, ed. *Zenkoku mukashibanashi kiroku: Sadojima mukashibanashi shū*. Tokyo: Sanseidō, 1942. Print.

Yoshida, Atsuhiko. *Mukashibanashi no kōkogaku* [Archeology of Folktales]. Tokyo: Chūō Kōronsha, 1992. Print.

Zeami, Motokiyo. "Yamamba." *Yōkyoku shū 2*. Shinpen nihon koten bungaku zenshū 59. Ed. Koyama Hiroshi and Satō Ken'ichiro. Tokyo: Shōgakukan, 1998. 564–622. Print.

Zipes, Jack. *Breaking the Magic Spell: Radical Theories of Folk and Fairy Tales*. Austin: U of Texas P, 1979. Print.

———. *The Irresistible Fairy Tale: The Cultural and Social History of a Genre*. Princeton: Princeton UP, 2012. Print.

———. *Relentless Progress: The Reconfiguration of Children's Literature, Fairy Tales, and Storytelling*. New York: Routledge, 2009. Print.

———, ed. *The Trials and Tribulations of Little Red Riding Hood*. 2nd ed. New York: Routledge, 1993. Print.

INDEX